BRITAIN'S WILD LARDER

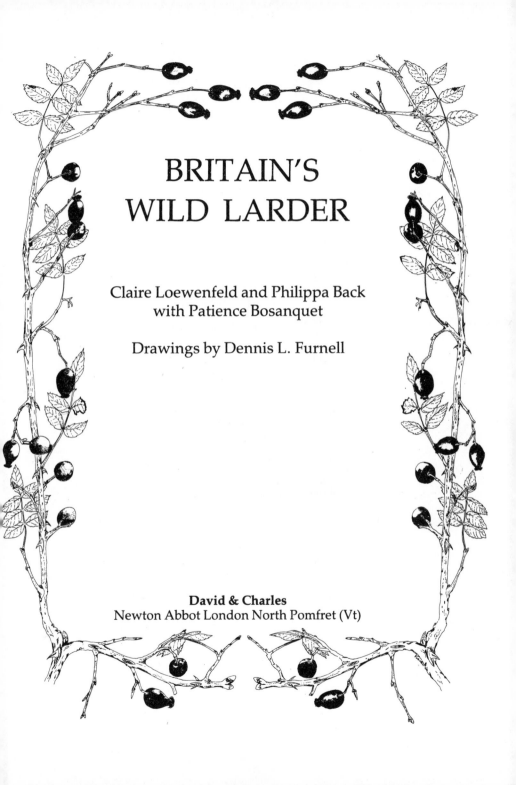

BRITAIN'S WILD LARDER

Claire Loewenfeld and Philippa Back
with Patience Bosanquet

Drawings by Dennis L. Furnell

David & Charles
Newton Abbot London North Pomfret (Vt)

British Library Cataloguing in Publication Data

Loewenfeld, Claire
    Britain's wild larder.
    1. Plants, Edible – Great Britain
    I. Title   II. Back, Philippa
    III. Bosanquet, Patience
    581.6'32'0941   QK98.5.G7

ISBN 0–7153–7971–2

Photoset, printed and bound in Great Britain
by Redwood Burn Limited, Trowbridge & Esher
for David & Charles (Publishers) Limited
Brunel House Newton Abbot Devon

Published in the United States of America
by David & Charles Inc
North Pomfret   Vermont 05053   USA

CONTENTS

1
FINDING PLANTS IN THE COUNTRYSIDE

Many of us are actively interested in the countryside and its wild plants. Most of us also enjoy trying new flavours in our cooking. To combine the two interests is a joy, and can be done without stripping the countryside of plants that need conservation – or eating anything unsuitable!

During the summer it is still possible to go for a walk in the country and gather, in an hour, sufficient wild foods to make a delicious nourishing soup or vegetable purée. The pleasure of searching for and identifying the plants adds enormously to the attractions of a ramble. The plants are wholesome and full of vitamins and the new flavours add variety to your daily diet. Blackberries, mushrooms and hazelnuts, good as they are, need not be regarded as the only wild foods fit for our tables.

You do need to have some idea where to look for food plants, and at what time of year you will find a particular plant: in every season there are some wild food plants ready to be gathered – see Chapter 9. Look for salad plants in early spring, when leaves are young and tender, by the sides of disused railway lines and along the verges, hedgerows and ditches of the small country lanes. All summer long you can find food plants, according to their species, on chalk hills and downland, on the edges of fields and by old buildings in undisturbed urban and country areas. Other plants can be found on marshlands and bogs and along the river banks, as well as by ponds and over common land.

Some fruits and berries can be found along the hedgerows, on the edges of woods and in copses. Others grow high up on exposed

7

Puff-balls: the small *perlatum* and the large *gigantum*

places, as on moorland heaths and rocky outcrops, where the vegetation is sparse but tough-growing. Look for plants where new road building has disturbed old pastures, bringing to the surface soil full of dormant seeds which start to grow again in new surroundings.

There are plants to be found along the seashore just above the high-tide mark which flourish in the salty air. For the edible seaweeds look along the seashore on rocks and in pools left exposed when the tide goes down. Other seaweeds grow only below the low-tide level but are easy to gather in wellington boots and with a pair of scissors.

To find the various species of mushroom and other edible fungi, search in pine forests and in deciduous woods, and in open fields where horses have been grazing and where the pasture has been left undisturbed for a few years.

In the late summer and early autumn begin gathering nuts. Most of the trees bearing edible nuts grow in a rich, loamy soil in woods and copses, and sometimes in ditches along the roadsides. Many a country lane is flanked by hazel-nut bushes which provide easy picking and make a thick impenetrable hedge.

Select your wild foods with care so as not to be disappointed. It is worthwhile picking only the best and ripest from a number of plants rather than picking in one spot and having to throw some away.

8

Nowadays it is necessary to emphasise the often damaging effect on wild food plants that the use of chemical sprays can have. Air, water and soil can all be polluted by artificial means. Those things which are not normally present in the environment and that have a biological effect on plants, animals and man can be said to be pollutants. One of the worst of those to affect plant life is car exhaust. On roads which carry a high concentration of traffic, much of the roadside vegetation is either killed or of stunted growth. The actual constituent of the fumes which causes the most damage to plants has not yet been isolated. But one of the hydrocarbons contained in exhaust is responsible for reducing the flowering of plants by fifty per cent.

Leaves of plants which are covered with oil and soot by passing traffic become clogged and cannot function properly, and on extremely busy roads some plants die through lack of light. Tree and plant life are also affected by the tons of salt which are spread on roads to free them of snow and ice in winter. When snow and ice melt, the salty water drains down into the verges. This can seriously inhibit the growth of trees in the area. The chemical sprays used in agriculture as insecticides can also damage plant life. So too can chemical fertilisers and the synthetic hormones used as selective weedkillers. Beware of picking plants in highly cultivated areas of land and in orchards.

There are many familiar and edible plants which if eaten in excess and over a long period of time can cause symptoms of poisoning: the spices nutmeg and coriander are examples. Other plants contain poisonous substances which can immediately be fatal or permanently damage health. It is important, therefore, when roaming the countryside that you are able to identify exactly those wild plants which contain the dangerous poisons. The following lists of poisonous plants and fungi are by no means comprehensive but they cover those most commonly found growing wild or in gardens throughout Britain:

FLOWERS AND TREES
Aconite/Monk's Hood/Wolfsbane (*Aconitum napellus*)
Foxglove (*Digitalis purpurea*)
Laburnum/Golden rain (*Cytisus laburnum*)
Autumn crocus/Meadow saffron (*Colchicum autumnale*)

Baneberry/Herb Christopher/Doll's eyes (*Actaea spicata*)
Deadly nightshade (*Atropa belladonna*)
English ivy (*Hedera helix*)
Common buckthorn (*Rhamnus catharticus*)
Cuckoo pint/Lords and ladies (*Arum maculatum*)
White bryony (*Bryonia dioica*)
Bittersweet/Woody nightshade (*Solanum dulcamara*)
Black bryony (*Tamus communis*)
Spindle tree (*Euonymus europaeus*)
Bracken (*Pteris aquilina*)
Spurge laurel (*Daphne laureola*)
Henbane (*Hyoscyamus niger*)
Fool's parsley (*Aethusa cynapium*)
Hemlock (*Conium maculatum*)
Buttercups/Crowfoots (*Ranunculus* species)
Corncockle (*Agrostemma githago*)
Stinking hellebore/Bear's foot (*Helleborus foetidus*)
Lily of the valley (*Convallaria majalis*)
Common privet (*Ligustrum vulgare*)
Celandine poppy/Greater celandine (*Chelidonium majus*)
Holly berries (*Ilex aquifolium*)
Honeysuckle berries (*Lonicera periclymenum*)
Ragwort (*Senecio jacobaea*)
Wild lupin (*Lupinus arboreus*)
Traveller's joy (*Clematis vitalba*)
Marsh marigold (*Caltha palustris*)
All spurges (*Euphorbia* var.)
Male fern (*Aspidium filix-mas*)

FUNGI
Yellow-staining mushroom (*Agaricus [psalliota] xanthodermus*)
Fly agaric (*Amanita muscaria*), and, related and very similar to fly
    agaric: *Amanita regalis*
Panther mushroom (*Amanita pantherina*)
Death cap (*Amanita phalloides*)
Destroying angel (*Amanita virosa*)
Blusher (*Amanita rubescens*)
Fool's mushroom (*Amanita verna*)
False death cap (*Amanita citrina*)

Devil's boletus (*Boletus satanus*)
Lurid boletus (*Boletus luridus*)
False morel (*Gyromitra (Helvella) esculenta*)
Hebeloma (*Hebeloma crustuliniforme*)
Sulphur tuft (*Hypholoma fasciculare*)
Red-staining inocybe (*Inocybe patouillardii*)

Other dangerous inocybes: *Inocybe fastiguata; I. lacera; I. greseo-lilacina; I. praetervisa; I. squamata; I. langei*
Woolly milkcap (*Lactarius torminosus*)

Other dangerous milkcaps: *Lactarius helvus; L. rufus*; Poisonous lepiota (*Lepiota helveola; L. fuscovinaceae*); Crested lepiota (*Lepiota cristata*); Mycena mushroom (*Mycena pura*); Paxillus (genus *Boletineae*) (*Paxillus involutus*); Leaden entoloma (*Rhodophyllus [Entoloma] sinatus*); Common earth ball (*Scleroderma aurantium*); Tiger blewit (*Tricholoma aurantium*)

Every plant grows best in its own particular environment with a right time for harvesting. Individual directions as to when and where to find the wild foods are given under each plant heading, but there are a number of general points about picking wild plants for food which are important.

1 The best time to pick the salad plants is usually in spring, when leaves are young and tender. Throughout the growing season, green leaves and stems can be picked for cooked vegetables. Roots too can be eaten in this way. Flowers are picked for salads as they appear. In the autumn the nuts, roots, stone fruits and berries can be harvested. It is also the time to look for field and woodland mushrooms and fungi.
2 Avoid picking plants from roadsides where weedkillers are likely to have been used.
3 Try to avoid gathering wild foods alongside roads which carry a lot of traffic, as fumes can contaminate the plants, spoiling their fragrance and flavour and reducing their food value. This especially applies to leaves and flowers.
4 Do not pick leafy food plants from verges or grassland along which dogs are constantly exercised.
5 In highly developed farming areas avoid picking plants in the

immediate vicinity of fields where insecticide sprays are likely to be used.

6 Never over-pick a plant, stripping it bare of leaves, fruit or nuts, otherwise it will not survive. Gather only the amount you need and always take especial care when digging up roots.

7 Try to avoid damaging the plants by breaking branches of trees and shrubs, or stems of green plants—in other words, gather with care.

8 In a good season the countryside provides a plentiful supply of wild foods which is there for the picking so select them carefully. Choose young leaves, whole and undamaged, whether for salads or cooking. Fruits should be insect-free with skin unbroken and perfectly ripe. Gather fruits and berries when they are dry in an open basket rather than a paper or polythene bag. The paper bag will soon fall to pieces and fruit or berries placed in a polythene bag will start to sweat and then spoil.

9 Wear gloves when picking fruit and berries from sharp-thorned plants. Use the handle of a walking stick gently to hook and lower the high branches and for holding back prickly stems so that you can reach the fruit more easily.

10 Use scissors when gathering leaves and flowers to avoid bruising and losing valuable vitamins and trace elements from the plant.

11 Gather mushrooms and other fungi in the early morning before the sun, wind and dust can penetrate their outer cover and dry them out. Pick fungi into open baskets and do not pile them too highly on top of one another.

12 Try to deal with them as quickly as possible after picking, whether they are to be eaten fresh, salted, pickled or dried.

13 If there is any doubt as to the identity of a plant being picked for eating it should be left strictly alone. Use books which give clear descriptions of the plants and are easy to understand. Coloured illustrations are an added help and important when looking for edible fungi. Use charts with at-a-glance information; these are light to carry and easy to follow. For mushrooms and other fungi the best way to learn how to distinguish between the edible and inedible ones is to go out with an experienced gatherer.

Conservation of wildlife, both plant and animal, is of great importance in a highly populated and industrialised country such as

Britain. To ensure the survival of all the different species, the countryside needs to be managed actively by specific organisations. These should be, and generally are, backed up by law in protecting those species most in danger of disappearing. The individual who wishes to enjoy wild foods from year to year, can do much to help.

First of all follow the Country Code and make sure gates are shut behind you. Always take your litter home with you. Fire is a real risk, especially during a dry spell of weather, so never throw a lighted cigarette-end into the grass. Walk round the edge of fields to avoid damage to hedgerows and farm crops, including pasture and fields of grass being left to grow for the hay harvest.

The countryside is criss-crossed with public footpaths and rights of way which are included on the large-scale Ordnance Survey maps. Often these footpaths go through the middle of a field in which case, if it has a standing crop on it, you cannot then use it. Local councils sometimes provide helpful maps for walkers, setting out different walks using public footpaths and including descriptions of where to go, what to see and how long each walk will take.

For those venturing into the countryside to gather wild foods, it is as well to know a little of the countryman's law. Trespass on private land is not a crime in itself but becomes one when an offence is committed, such as digging up a plant for removal, which is stealing, trampling on a growing crop or breaking or damaging a hedge or fence. It is perfectly legal to gather wild blackberries and the owner can neither prosecute the picker nor demand the pickings since wild food is considered a natural product of the soil and has no owner until it is gathered.

Wild plants first came under the protection of the law in 1975 when twenty-one species of rare plants were included in the Conservation of Wild Creatures and Wild Plants Act. These plants are protected against picking, uprooting or destruction. The Act states that it is illegal, except in certain special circumstances, for anyone who is not authorised to uproot any wild plant without reasonable excuse.

Under the terms of the Act an authorised person means the owner or occupier of the land or anyone who has his permission. The Act is intended mainly to stop collectors from decimating rare plant species. Fines of up to £200 can be imposed on anyone guilty of offences under the Act.

The twenty-one plants in danger of extinction and protected by the law are the following:

Alpine gentian (*Gentiana nivalis*)
Alpine sowthistle (*Cicerbita alpina*)
Alpine woodsia (*Woodsia alpina*)
Blue heath (*Phyllodoce caerulea*)
Cheddar pink (*Dianthus gratianopolitanus*)
Diapensia (*Diapensia lapponica*)
Drooping saxifrage (*Saxifraga cernua*)
Ghost orchid (*Epipogium aphyllum*)
Killarney fern (*Trichomanes speciosum*)
Lady's slipper (*Cypripedium calceolus*)
Mezereon (*Daphne mezereun.*)
Military orchid (*Orchis militaris*)
Monkey orchid (*Orchis simia*)
Oblong woodsia (*Woodsia ilvensis*)
Red helleborine (*Cephalanthera rubra*)
Snowdon lily (*Lloydia serotina*)
Spiked speedwell (*Veronica spicata*)
Spring gentian (*Gentiana verna*)
Teesdale sandwort (*Minuartia stricta*)
Tufted saxifrage (*Saxifraga cespitosa*)
Wild gladiolus (*Gladiolus illyricus*)

These plants must not be picked at any time. This law can only be effective if supported by informed public opinion.

There are a number of societies and organisations concerned with the protection and preservation of wildlife and countryside in Britain. Heading the list are the official organisations sponsored by the government:

NATURE CONSERVANCY COUNCIL
Established in 1973, the Council is responsible for the conservation of flora, fauna, geological and physiographical features throughout Great Britain and for establishing, maintaining and managing National Nature Reserves. It is a source of advice and information for all whose activities affect the natural environment. To these

ends it commissions, supports and undertakes relevant research and can also give grants for the carrying out of any project within its sphere of interest.

COUNTRYSIDE COMMISSION
The Commission provides and improves facilities for the enjoyment of the countryside in England and Wales. It designates National Parks and areas of outstanding natural beauty, submits proposals for long-distance footpaths and bridleways, recommends grants, and encourages the provision of country parks and picnic sites.

COUNTRYSIDE COMMISSION FOR SCOTLAND
Set up in 1967 for the provision, development and improvement of facilities for the enjoyment of the Scottish countryside, and for the conservation and enhancement of its natural beauty and amenity.

FORESTRY COMMISSION
The Commission is responsible for promoting the interests of forestry in Great Britain. It implements legislation concerning tree health, felling licences, woodlands etc. It has developed the recreational potential and amenity importance of some of its forests, establishing forest parks to which the public are admitted.

The principal voluntary organisations are the following:

BOTANICAL SOCIETY OF THE BRITISH ISLES
The Society is concerned with the study of the systematics and distribution of flowering plants and ferns, and supports all measures to conserve them.

BRITISH NATURALISTS' ASSOCIATION
The Association aims to encourage communication between naturalists in Great Britain and overseas. It supports schemes for the improvement of wildlife, the preservation of natural beauty, and the promotion and maintenance of National Parks, nature reserves and conservation areas.

BRITISH TRUST FOR CONSERVATION VOLUNTEERS
An organisation concerned with the conservation and maintenance

of the character and amenity of rural and urban areas. It runs and finances a voluntary field force, the National Conservation Corps, and tries to educate the public, young people in particular, in the principles and practice of nature conservation.

COMMONS, OPEN SPACES AND FOOTPATHS PRESERVATION SOCIETY
Its aims are to preserve commons and village greens for public use, to advise on the securing and preserving of public open spaces, to obtain public access to open country and to preserve footpaths and bridleways. It offers legal advice on matters within its scope to local authorities, Commons committees, voluntary bodies, individual members and the general public.

COUNTY NATURALISTS' TRUSTS
Every county in England and Wales has a Naturalists' Trust which establishes and manages nature reserves, organises meetings, lectures and visits for its members and publishes newsletters and other items. Many of the trusts arrange working parties amongst their members to carry out a range of nature-conservation tasks on their nature reserves during weekends.

FIELD STUDIES COUNCIL
It encourages the pursuit of field work and research in all branches of knowledge whose essential subject matter is out of doors.

FRIENDS OF THE EARTH
The primary objectives are to promote understanding and appreciation of the need for conservation and preservation of natural resources and natural beauty.

NATIONAL TRUST
The Trust owns and safeguards for the nation considerable areas of the most beautiful countryside and unspoilt coastline in England, Wales and Northern Ireland.

NATIONAL TRUST FOR SCOTLAND
Performs the same function in Scotland.

16

RAMBLERS' ASSOCIATION

It seeks to encourage rambling and mountaineering, to foster a greater knowledge, love and care of the countryside, and works for the preservation of natural beauty, the protection of footpaths, and the provision of access to open country.

SOCIETY FOR THE PROMOTION OF NATURE CONSERVATION
(ASSOCIATION OF NATURE CONSERVATION TRUSTS)

Seeks to promote the conservation, study and appreciation of nature, and protection of flora and fauna, by creating and establishing nature reserves representing typical natural and semi-natural habitats. It provides a co-ordinating centre for the independent trusts, administering funds and providing practical advice on conservation to public and private bodies.

THE WOODLAND TRUST

Aims to conserve, restore and re-establish trees, and in particular broadleaved trees, plants and all forms of wildlife in the United Kingdom of Great Britain and Northern Ireland, and thereby to secure and enhance the enjoyment by the public of the natural environment of those territories.

2
HOW TO USE WILD PLANTS AS FOOD

In addition to the satisfaction of obtaining something for nothing, there is considerable nutritional value in indigenous wild foods to enrich and supplement the daily diet. After the winter, vegetables and salad foods become scarce and expensive, giving an added incentive to search for the first wild greenery. You also benefit from the fresh air and exercise which can involve the whole family.

There is more goodness in a plant which grows unmolested by chemical fertilisers and other pollutants than in a great many so-called fresh foods. Wild plants, unlike cultivated crops, will thrive on poorer land, in woods, hedgerows and on waste ground. Healthy food plants contain a natural balance of nutrients acquired from a healthy soil. Loss of nutrients by factory processing and the additions of various chemicals to the food destroy the natural balance. A diet consisting mainly of this kind of denatured food is thought to be linked to many chronic and degenerative diseases.

Nearly all nutrients needed to maintain health are contained in the green leaves, stalks, flowers, seeds and roots of edible green plants, in fruits and berries, nuts and mushrooms and some sea-weeds. The plants, many of which we call weeds and tend to destroy, are full of chlorophyll and sap, rich in vitamins, minerals and other active substances.

Vegetable protein, obtainable from nuts, green leaves and mush-rooms, is essential for growth and maintenance of health. Nuts, with their many culinary uses, are a concentrated food with a low water content. For example, hazelnuts contain more protein, fat and carbohydrates than eggs. They also contain more minerals than cow's milk and are richer in vitamins B1 and C. Animal protein could well be reduced in your diet if you combine wild plants, mushrooms, nuts and fruit to give a high content of essential nutrients.

Vitamins and mineral elements regulate, regenerate and maintain the body and its mechanisms, helping to resist infections. A clear skin and healthy hair depend on them. Vitamins, especially vitamin C, are abundant in wild fruits and berries, also in nuts, fungi and green plants. Minerals and trace elements are in all wild foods. Seaweeds are a source of iodine, not found in many other plants; they also contain the vitamins P and K, a factor in blood clotting.

Carbohydrates, the starches and sugars, provide the body with energy. Good sources are nuts, seeds and various roots, tubers, corms, bulbs, rhizomes and rootstocks. These underground parts of

Hazel-nuts and catkins

19

plants, if prepared and cooked correctly, also provide some vitamin C, protein and fibre. Fibre, the essential roughage, mostly lacking in modern refined foods, is needed in the diet to keep the system healthy and avoid constipation—the root cause of a long list of related disorders.

Fats and oils, necessary for energy and the body's absorption of the fat-soluble vitamins, are provided by the autumn crop of hazelnuts, beechnuts, walnuts and sweet almonds. Extracting oil from nuts can be difficult; the best way to make use of the valuable unsaturated fats and oils contained in nuts is to include them in the diet for their ideal combination of nutritious calories.

Improving your daily diet

In December and January there are one or two plants with green leaves to cheer up winter menus. From February onwards it is possible to find a greater variety of fresh wild food. A daily raw salad

Burdock

20

will provide most of the necessary vitamins for the family, and when the plants are young use leaves, flower tops, stems and roots. Welcome extra vitamins and minerals can be found in chickweed, cornsalad, daisy, dandelion, purslane, brooklime, scurvy grass and samphire. Mix them with other salad greens and add thinly sliced roots of yellow goatsbeard, sow thistle and hawkbit. Toss the salad in a simple oil and lemon-juice dressing flavoured with a tablespoon of mixed wild herbs. The oil in the dressing is important for the body's absorption of the fat-soluble vitamins in the green leaves. If lemons are scarce, try the vinegary leaves of common sorrel or wood sorrel instead. Edible flowers add their colour and flavour to a salad.

Nettles, dandelions, docks, sorrel, fat hen, purslane, sea beet and ground elder make an excellent kind of spinach, either as a vegetable on their own or mixed with cultivated spinach. Stripped of their leaves, which need very little time to cook, the stems, stalks, midribs and shoots of plants such as samphire, seakale, milk thistle and burdock, make asparagus-like vegetables. Substitutes for root vegetables and potatoes can be found growing wild: salsify, great burdock, marsh woundwort, some thistles, silverweed, willowherb and the starchy tubers of the earthnut (*Carum bulbocastanum*) are examples. Some roots are sweet-flavoured; others such as dandelion roots can be dried, roasted and ground to powder as a coffee substitute or for adding to bought coffee.

The distinctive volatile oils in the many wild herbs give their characteristic flavours to stimulate the appetite. Look for wild mint, thyme, marjoram, fennel, parsley and sage. Many provide seasonings and substitute condiments, adding zest and interest to salads, salad dressings, stews, dumplings, fritters and puddings. Wild chervil, the first umbellifer to appear in spring, can take the place of parsley in all recipes; wild garlic (ramsons) and Jack-by-the-hedge provide a mild garlic flavour. Other wild herbs such as goatsbeard stems and sweet cicely can be used as sweeteners.

The wonderful summer fruits and berries provide vitamin-rich sweets and desserts, preserves and home-made drinks. Rosehips contain more vitamin C than any other plant growing wild, and they store well in dried or puréed form for winter menus.

From Britain's seashores the mineral-rich seaweeds provide unusual vegetables, flavours and a gelatine substitute or thickening agent.

21

Nuts, a source of natural, unprocessed starch, protein and fat, are a non-acid food. Nuts are good raw, chopped in salads, used for savoury sandwich fillings and spreads, in hot and cold sweets and all sweet baking and confectionery. Chestnuts contain little oil and are easy to digest; they should always be cooked. Finely ground hazelnuts can be mixed with flour in baking, or can replace it completely. Sweet almonds make a nutritious nutmilk, good for children's drinks and in cooking (see page 160).

Wild mushrooms and fungi are full of nutrients and contain more protein and carbohydrates than most vegetables. Unlike other plants they also contain vitamin D. Some people find mushrooms indigestible but if prepared and cooked with care, wild fungi can enrich and flavour food in the many ways suggested for the individual species.

Flavours and textures of wild plants

All wild vegetables have stronger flavours and tougher fibres than cultivated varieties. Pick young tender leaves, shoots and stalks. Try to combine the different flavours—neutral, mild, strong, sweet, bitter and acid—so that no single flavour dominates a mixture. Make *bouquets garnis* from a mixture of wild chervil, thyme, sage, ramsons or Jack-by-the-hedge. Tie the herbs in a muslin bag and remove it after flavouring a sauce, soup or stock.

Some of the wild green vegetables with a strong or tart flavour can be blanched before cooking, although this may cause them to lose valuable vitamins and minerals, especially iron. Young stalks should be crisp enough to eat raw, but the older stems will need peeling. Wild strawberries, raspberries and blackberries are often sweet enough to use on their own. Most other wild fruits are acid in varying degrees and require cooking or preserving.

The flavour of wild mushrooms and other fungi differs from that of the cultivated mushrooms. Some have a nutty, radishy or clove-like taste, others are peppery, mealy or have their own distinctive aromatic flavour. Field mushrooms, boleti, morels and chanterelles have the best flavours for using on their own; all other kinds can be mixed, and blend well together.

Most seaweeds have a distinct salty taste due to the iodine they contain, but they are nutritious vegetables and free! They require

Morels

special preparation and cooking as described in Chapter 6.

Nuts have their own individual flavours. Raw or cooked, hazelnuts, sweet almonds and walnuts blend well with other wild foods and can be interchanged in most nut recipes.

Preparing and Cooking

Wild foods need careful preparation to make the most of them. Eat them raw whenever possible; many young leaves and roots are suitable for mixing into salads and sandwiches; wild fruits, nuts and mushrooms may also be eaten raw. Nutrients are lost from the moment of picking, for instance as much as 40 per cent of vitamin C after 24 hours. Vitamins are also reduced by shredding or grating, soaking in cold water or adding bicarbonate of soda to the cooking water. Colour and flavour are lost by bad cooking, so prepare and eat the food as soon after collection as possible. Pressure cooking is a good method provided it is not overdone—all too easy with tender leaves.

WILD VEGETABLES

Gather the plants just before cooking. Wash leaves quickly in luke-

23

warm water and shake dry; pat between towels if needed for salad. Roots may need to be gently scrubbed. Peel or scrape stems and cut into equal lengths. To cook: steam or cook young greens gently in a little stock, water or fat for a few minutes until tender. The vegetables can also be puréed and used in the different ways suggested for nettles. Tie stems in bundles and boil or steam as for the green vegetables. They may also be cooked slowly in the oven in a little fat with herbs and vegetable broth, sprinkled with grated cheese and sour cream.

Soup is an ideal way of using mixed wild vegetables and herbs. For extra nourishment include finely cubed potatoes, pasta or rice and serve with grated cheese. Wild sorrel and nettle make good soups on their own. To preserve nutrients use wild vegetables and roots in a stew or casserole, in steamed vegetable puddings, dumplings, croquettes, stuffings and forcemeats.

To save fuel, try fuelless cooking in a haybox or vacuum flask. The principle of the haybox is to bring the food to boiling point. Place the food in a heavy, lidded pot or casserole in a well-insulated box. The pot is then wrapped or covered with more insulation and the box closed. The food cooks slowly overnight and only requires heating up before serving. This is a good way of avoiding long use of the oven for stews and casseroles.

A haybox should consist of a stout, well-made wooden box with a tight-fitting lid. Line the inside with kitchen foil, then a thick layer of hay or other insulating material, packing it in so that only a space remains to fit the chosen pot. Cover it with a cushion filled with more hay or insulation to fit the top. An old rug or blanket wrapped round the pot will also do, but the hay must be reshaped and it is still advisable to add a further layer of insulation before closing the box.

A vacuum flask works in the same way but will only take small quantities of foods such as fruit, young leaves etc, brought to the boil, sealed in the flask and left for several hours.

WILD FRUIT
Ripe wild strawberries, raspberries and blackberries are best eaten raw, lightly washed and eaten as soon after picking as possible. These sweet fruits are good for adding to breakfast muesli for a vitamin-rich start to the day. Raw wild strawberry jam can be made

24

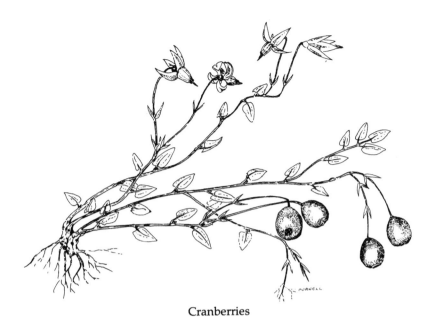

Cranberries

using equal weights of fruit and sugar (see page 67). Other fruits
need sweetening before eating. Barberries, bilberries and rowan-
berries give a pleasant acidity and unusual flavour to fat meats. Put
a handful of raw berries on top of a joint for the last half hour of
cooking so that their juices run into the meat.

Most wild fruits make delicious purées, preserves and drinks for
storing. Haws, elderberries, cranberries and crab apples all make
good jellies, on their own or in combination. Follow the basic
method for jelly-making in this chapter. Try the wild fruit jam recipe
using different fruits and ground hazelnuts on page 172.

The prolific autumn crop of rosehips is well worth the time and
effort it takes to prepare them. Remove their prickly hairs, top, tail
and wash the hips in lukewarm water. Put them into a stainless-
steel or enamel pan and cover with boiling water. Bring back to the
boil and simmer with lid on for 15 minutes, then purée the hips.
This purée, full of vitamin C, can be used in a variety of ways given
on page 62. Unusual recipes for sauces, sweets and desserts, pies,
puddings and lovely home-made ice cream, and other suggestions
for using them, are given for the individual wild fruits concerned.

For raw fruit juices allow 100–125g (4–5oz) of fruit per person. Put through a juice presser or an electric juice extractor. Dilute with water and sweeten if necessary. Fruit syrups, vinegars and wines can also be made; follow the directions on pages 34–6.

When cooking fruits, use stainless steel, glazed earthenware or enamel pans, avoiding aluminium if possible. Stir or mash the fruit with clean wooden or stainless-steel spoons.

NUTS

All nuts require shelling and skinning. Roast hazelnuts in a hot oven for 10–20 minutes, shaking occasionally. Take out and roll nuts in a cloth to rub off skins. To remove sweet almond skins, blanch them in boiling water. Use them to make nut cream or nut milk by pounding the nuts with a little water in a mortar and pestle or an electric liquidizer. Dilute with water or fruit juice, or use undiluted in place of rich cream. Hazelnuts, almonds and walnuts can be eaten raw, roasted, chopped or ground to a meal in a nut mill, mouli grater or electric or rotary grinder. Sweet chestnuts should not be eaten raw. To shell and peel chestnuts, cut slits on the flat side of the nuts. Throw about a dozen nuts into boiling water for a few minutes. Take out a few at a time to shell and peel, leaving the others in the simmering water. Alternatively, cut slits as before but bake on a tin in a hot oven for 5–10 minutes until the shell splits, when it is easily removed with a knife. See the recipes and suggestions for using under the names of the individual nuts.

WILD MUSHROOMS AND FUNGI

All varieties should be used as soon after picking as possible, but may be stored for a short time in a closed container in the fridge.

Wild mushrooms

To prepare: trim away inedible parts, remove tip of stem to check for signs of burrowing insects. Wipe off grit and grass with damp cloth. If further washing is necessary rinse quickly under tap, drain and pat dry with cloth or kitchen paper. To cook: follow directions for cultivated varieties. They can also be grilled, cooked on a spit, or stuffed, but first remove stalks. Slice mushrooms raw, or use them cooked in salads. They provide an excellent flavour for ketchups and are good for freezing, drying or bottling.

26

Boleti and ceps
To prepare: unless perfect young specimens, the soft tubes should be removed, using sound caps and stems only. Brush gently or rinse under tap. The more spongy varieties of boleti, eg *B.luteus* or *B.granulatus*, should not be washed; peel cap and remove the tubes. To cook: large ceps and boleti are best cut into slices as a vegetable, or added to a stew. Grill them for a few minutes to get rid of the water before using in a recipe. All these fungi are good for preserving by any method.

Blewits including *St George's mushroom*
To prepare: fragile and watery so collect on dry days. Trim and remove woody stem. Wipe clean. To cook: stew in butter or other fat. Add to vegetable stews or serve in a white sauce. Good for drying, bottling etc.

Chanterelles including *horn of plenty*
To prepare: trim and wash well under tap. Drain thoroughly. To cook: traditionally with eggs. Slice and fry quickly. Do not roast or stew or they will become tough. Good mixed with morels and boleti. Horn of plenty is best when dried for flavouring.

Saffron milk caps
To prepare: check that the 'milk' is orange red and *not* white. Choose only sound specimens. Trim and wash as for others. To cook: never stew, as an unpleasant flavour develops. Best fried quickly or in casseroles. In salads, boil caps for few minutes, cool and slice.

Parasols
To prepare: use young caps only of large varieties. Discard stalks. Scrape but do not wash the caps. To cook: Do not overcook. Halve, egg and breadcrumb, or dip in batter and fry quickly. Cook in butter like mushrooms; steam and serve on toast.

Shaggy and ink caps
To prepare: only edible when young and the gills pink. Cut off stalks, peel cap off downwards. Use only large ones when their 'umbrella' cap is still tightly folded. To cook: dip in batter and shal-

low or deep fry. Bake or stew slowly in a casserole. Stuff with chopped stewed fungi.

Morels

To prepare: reject soft or watery specimens. Important to wash well, changing water several times to remove grit from small surface openings. Then boil for a few minutes in slightly salted water, drain and pat dry. To cook: cut up in slices, dip in batter and fry or bake. Stuff or use as filling for pancakes. Do not eat too many morels at one time. Good fungi for drying.

Puffballs

To prepare: only good when young. Flesh must be white. Always peel. To cook: large kinds, cut and fry, coated or plain. Small ones, deep-fry whole, drain and sprinkle with salt. All kinds are good in fungi mixtures.

Preserving

Preserve wild food by freezing, drying or bottling; with sugar for jams and jellies, fruit juice and syrups; with vinegar and spices for pickles, chutneys, ketchups, purées, relishes and bottled sauces; with yeast or alcohol for wines, beers, home-made liqueurs and infusions. Foods such as nuts and some roots can be stored without any processing.

FREEZING

Most freezer manufacturers give general directions for preparing and freezing food. It is important to get the food to the freezer as quickly as possible after picking and preparing. When closing containers for the freezer see that lids fit well, or if food is in polythene bags, extract the air before sealing. When the food is needed take it out in time to allow it to thaw slowly at room temperature.

Wild fruits and berries

Gather fruits for freezing on a dry day. Pick over, discard imperfect fruit, and if necessary wash quickly in a colander and drain. Spread fruit or berries out on a large platter or plastic tray that will fit in the freezer and place it uncovered in the coldest part for an hour or so.

When frozen put fruit into polythene bags or other containers and return to freezer. Fruits for desserts are improved by the addition of dry sugar mixed with the fruit before freezing, or in a cold sugar syrup. Purée over-ripe fruit, sweeten to taste and then freeze. Fruit juices can also be frozen, and these as well as purées need at least ½in air space at the top of the container to allow for expansion.

Wild vegetables and plants
Only the leaves, stems and roots for cooked vegetables are suitable for freezing. Salad greens go limp. Gather the plants on a dry day when they are perfect for eating, prepare and put immediately into polythene bags, stalks and all. Close and freeze. Freeze small-leafed plants and flavouring herbs in bunches. Chop herbs, put them in ice-cube trays and fill up with water or clear strong stock. Freeze the tray and when hard take out cubes, wrap individually and pack into bags. Return to freezer. This can be done with single herbs or better still, a mixture for using in soups, stews, sauces and gravies.

Root vegetables
Slice and blanch root vegetables for the freezer in boiling water for 2 minutes, cool immediately and drain before packing into containers. Blanching prevents deterioration through enzyme action. For spinach-type plants, pick leaves when young, wash and blanch for 1 minute. Cool, press out excess moisture and pack into polythene bags as before.

Nuts
Shelled nuts keep well for long periods in the freezer. Use whole, chopped or milled nuts and wrap in convenient quantities, taking the usual precautions to exclude air from the packets.

DRYING
This method preserves the food by removing most or all of the moisture while retaining colour and aroma. When needed for cooking, the addition of liquid restores the flavour. This is usually stronger than the fresh product.

1 Use a special drying cabinet constructed to take layers of stacking trays placed over an electric or other heater. The fan type is best

29

to circulate the warm air. The trays need a mesh base which can be nylon, muslin or cheesecloth.

2 Spread out the food to be dried on trays with a mesh base and place in an oven at its lowest temperature for an hour or longer according to thickness and water content of food; or place in a warm airing cupboard or dark boiler room.

3 Plants for vegetables or flavouring may be dried in bunches tied up by the stems and hung up, heads down, in a warm, dark place until the leaves are crisp but still green.

4 Foods such as mushrooms can be threaded on string or thin sticks and hung up as for vegetables in 3 above, or laid across the oven shelves and dried at low heat, turning them over occasionally.

Plants and herbs
Pick the plants for drying before they flower, and choose a dry sunless day. Spread them out on trays, or loosely tie in small bunches for hanging up, putting a sheet of clean paper beneath to catch any falling leaves. If drying in the oven it is necessary to leave the oven door ajar to maintain the low heat required and to provide ventilation. When correctly dried, leaves should be crisp, crumbly, and easily stripped off the stalks by hand. They will still be green and aromatic.

Store the crumbled leaves without pressing down in earthenware jars or glass bottles with screw tops. Keep glass containers away from light or mask them with big labels. But always label preserved food before storing.

Roots
Give roots a longer time at a slightly higher temperature to remove moisture. Clean and cut up before spreading out on trays. Turn them over once or twice until they are hard and brittle. Another method for root vegetables is to store them in sand or clamps as for the cultivated kinds. Clamps are made in the open and are normally used for storing the potato or carrot crops. The roots or tubers are heaped into a pyramid, covered with a thick thatch of straw and then 9in (22cm) of soil, leaving an opening at the top of the pyramid for a 'chimney' of straw to give ventilation. This should protect the food against frost damage and keep it in good condition until needed. To store roots in sand, simply lay them in boxes and cover

with a layer of fine sand. Store in a dry shed. Check frequently and discard spoiled roots.

Fruits

Only a few wild fruits are worth drying. Haws are an example as they can be ground into a flour for bread making. Dried bilberries and elderberries make a good substitute for currants. Rosehips should be cut in half lengthwise, spread out on a clean surface or trays and dried in low heat. They should remain bright red if correctly dried, overheating makes them go brown and lose aroma and vitamins. Next, shake the dried hips in a closed wire container to remove hairs, take out pips and store rosehips in earthenware or similar containers in the dark. Use the dried hips for making recipes suggested on page 62.

Mushrooms

Choose fresh firm specimens. Remove hard stems, peel if recommended for cooking, spread out on trays or thread on to string or stick. Dry as for plants but do not allow heat to exceed 100°C (200°F). Store in clean, tightly sealed glass jars and keep away from light. For powdered fungi, make sure they are completely dry and brittle before grinding in a pestle and mortar, nut mill, electric blender or grinder.

BOTTLING

Food preserved by bottling is first sterilised by heating and then vacuum sealed to prevent entry of air and micro-organisms during storage. Special bottles are available, but jam jars can be re-used provided they have screw-on lids that will form a seal. The preserving liquid can be plain water, salt water (brine) or sweetened water (syrup). The most suitable wild foods for preserving in this way are fruits and berries. Strawberries, raspberries and blackberries may also be rolled in castor sugar and bottled without liquid, then sterilised. The berries shrink but their taste remains wonderful. Most fruits can be puréed before bottling and sterilising, a good way of using over-ripe fruit. Mushrooms may be bottled in brine, but only the pressure-cooker method is recommended (page 32). For the brine, boil together 1 tablespoon cooking salt and 1.1 litres (2 pints) of water.

1 Deep pan (cold)

Fill bottles with fruit, pack tightly without bruising and fill to the top. Pour cold water or syrup over fruit and secure cap. Screw bands should always be loosened by a quarter or half turn to prevent bottles bursting. Place bottles in a large deep saucepan or fish kettle with a false base and well-fitting lid. The base can be a wire rack, a home-made wooden trellis, some straw or a rough cloth. Special sterilising pans are available and these have lids with built-in thermometers for accurate timing and temperatures. Make sure the bottles are not touching, then cover them with water and fit lid onto pan. Heat the water slowly from cold to simmering point in about 1½ hours over low heat and simmer for 15 minutes. Remove jars one by one on to a wooden surface to prevent cracking. If screw bands are used, screw them up tightly. Leave jars for 24 hours before testing for seal.

2 Deep pan (hot)

Use boiling liquid to fill bottles, stand them in the pan without touching, cover with warm water 40°C (100°F) and bring to simmering point in 30 minutes over high heat. Maintain at simmering for 2–5 minutes. Proceed as for method 1.

3 Pressure cooker

This is the most economical method. Fill bottles to within an inch of rim with boiling liquid. Stand them on rack in cooker without touching. The amount of water in cooker varies with the size and make, but there should be at least an inch before rack and bottles are put in. Secure lid, bring to boil and allow steam to escape from vent in a steady stream before closing and bringing pressure up to 5lb per square inch. Do not allow this process to take more than 5 minutes. Maintain pressure for 1 minute for most fruits, or the time recommended in maker's instructions. Take pan off heat immediately and allow pressure to reduce and pan to cool, about 10 minutes. Remove bottles one at a time and proceed as for deep-pan method.

4 Oven (dry method)

Pack the fruit into jars, cover with foil to prevent scorching, and place in the oven on a sheet of wood or cardboard, or a baking tin covered with several layers of newspaper. Turn oven on to 120°C (250°F, Gas ½) and leave jars in for 1–1¼ hours, or until beads of juice show on fruit. Take jars out one at a time. stand them on wooden surface and fill to top of each jar with boiling syrup or water. Close jar with lid according to type used. Tighten bands.

5 Oven (wet method)

Fill jars with fruit and cover with cold syrup or water. Put on lids and bands remembering not to tighten screw bands more than half a turn. Stand jars on a baking tin on folded newspaper and put in oven on bottom shelf. Turn heat to 135°C (275°F, Gas 1) and leave jars in for 1–1½ hours. Proceed as for dry method.

JAMS AND JELLIES

Gather, prepare and cook the fruit on the same day. If possible mix ripe and unripe fruit for best results. Pick over, discard unsound fruit, wash and drain. Remove only larger stems and leaves when making jelly. Hard-skinned fruits require cooking in water to cover in the preserving pan. Soft fruits need very little water or none at all, but crush the fruit in the pan and heat gently until the juice flows. Add lemon juice or other acid if required. Simmer fruit until soft, approximately ¾–1 hour, breaking up the fruit further if necessary to release the pectin.

For jellies, pour the cooked fruit into a clean jelly bag and suspend it over a bowl. Leave to drip. For a clear jelly do not squeeze the bag, although this produces more liquid and does not detract from the taste. Next, measure the juice and weigh the correct amount of sugar given in the recipe. For most fruit jellies as well as jams, this is equal measure for weight, except for low-pectin fruit which requires less sugar. Return juice to the pan and bring to boil.

At this point the procedure for jellies and jams is the same. Add the sugar to juice or cooked fruit and stir until dissolved. Boil rapidly without stirring for approximately 10 minutes, or until setting point is reached. To test, put a little hot liquid on to a saucer and allow to cool. Setting point is reached when the surface wrinkles if pushed or the saucer tilted. Another way is to dip a wooden spoon into the boiling jam or jelly, hold it for a moment to cool slightly, then allow the liquid to drip from the edge of the spoon. The drops will run together and break away in flakes if setting point has been reached. Special jam-making thermometers are available and simplify this process. The temperature should reach 105°C (220°F) for a good set. Do not overboil, as it will become too stiff and jellies will turn dark.

Take pan from heat, remove scum. Pour jellies while still hot into warm jars. Jams can be left to cool slightly before potting to prevent the fruit rising in the jars. Cover surface of hot jam or jelly with waxed paper discs. Tie down or put on lids, taking care with jellies not to tilt jars until cold.

CANDY AND SWEETMEATS

Many nuts, stems and fruits of the wild larder can be preserved in sugar. See candied burdock stems (p72) and candied chestnuts (p166). Walnuts and cooked chestnuts keep well when coated with stiffly whisked white of egg, rolled in sugar and dried off in a low oven. Store them in a tin or screwtop jar.

Sweetmeats for the store cupboard can be made from fruit. Cook fruits in a little water until very tender. Sieve the pulp, return to pan and add an equal weight of sugar. Cook over gentle heat until very thick, stirring all the time. Pour onto shallow tins or baking sheets lined with greaseproof paper. Leave in a warm place, in temperature not exceeding 40°C (120°F) for 2–3 days. When dry, peel off the paper, cut into small rounds and roll in castor sugar. Store in tins between layers of greaseproof paper.

FRUIT DRINKS AND VINEGARS

Wild fruits can be preserved as juices, syrups or vinegars.

Juice

Soften the ripe fruit by heating in a basin over a pan of boiling water, crushing the fruit until the juice runs. Alternatively ferment the pounded fruit in a jar until bubbles appear on the surface. To extract the juice use an electric juice extractor, or press the fruit through a nylon or hair sieve or a muslin cloth.

Syrup

Sweeten juice to retain flavour using 350g (¾lb) sugar to each 575ml (1pt) of juice, but twice this quantity is necessary if sterilising is to be avoided. For the smaller amount of sugar, sterilise by any of the methods described for bottling.

Vinegar

Fruit vinegars make unusual bases for hot or cold drinks. Blackberries, cranberries and barberries are good fruits to use. Add wine vinegar to the fruit in a large earthenware jar, cover with a cloth and leave to stand for 4–10 days, stirring occasionally. Blackberries need only 4 days without stirring. Strain the juice, measure and add 450g (1lb) sugar for every pint of juice. Bring to the boil, cook for 10–20 minutes according to recipe, removing scum as it rises. Take off heat and when quite cold pour into bottles. Cork, seal and store in a cool cupboard. The addition of a little brandy to the vinegar when it is cold makes a very special drink.

CHUTNEYS AND PICKLES

Preserve the fruit or vegetables using vinegar flavoured with spices and other seasoning. Cut up ingredients finely and cook slowly for 2 hours or longer. See bullace chutney, page 46.

Pickle tiny mushrooms in white wine vinegar flavoured with mace, salt, white pepper, ground ginger and a very little chopped onion. Cook slowly in a lidded pan until the mushrooms shrink, transfer to bottles or jars and cover with the strained vinegar. Cover and seal. For elderflower pickles see page 53. For samphire pickle see page 99.

KETCHUPS, SAUCES AND RELISHES

Use the same ingredients as chutneys but sieve or blend them after cooking. Elderberries make a delicious ketchup. Try mushroom relish, using wild fungi which are first broken up, put in a bowl, sprinkled with salt and left for 3–4 days. Then mash or pulp, add vinegar and spices and simmer for ½ hour. Strain and pour while hot into clean bottles and seal. Finally sterilise bottles in a pan of water kept simmering for ½ hour. (See recipe page 137.)

WINES AND BEERS

Many wines and beers can be made from wild fruits and plants, roots, flowers, leaves and young shoots. No special equipment is needed, but you will need a large bucket or container, butter muslin or other strainer, a fermentation lock, a funnel, bottles and clean corks. Avoid using containers made of iron, copper, zinc, lead or brass as these metals react with fruit acids and spoil the taste.

Wines

Pour water to cover onto the prepared fruit, flowers or leaves and leave for three days, stirring occasionally. Cover with a cloth and leave in an even temperature for 10–14 days until a crust forms on top. Yeast can be added to speed up this process; soften a little yeast, spread it on a piece of toast and float it, yeast side down, on top of the fermenting liquid.

Next, skim, strain through butter muslin or other strainer and measure the liquid. Additional flavouring or citric fruit juices can now be added, together with the sugar in the recipe. Stir in sugar until dissolved, but if heating the liquid do not let it get above blood heat or the yeast will be killed. Strain into jars, cask or bottles, reserving a little for 'topping up'. Cover jars or bottles—paper cups are good for this—or use a special fermentation lock. A home-made lock can be made from glass tubing threaded through a cork. Leave wine in a warm place for about 14 days until it has finished working, filling up with the reserve as liquid runs over if not using the lock covering.

Finally, pour carefully into clean bottles and cork down. All wines need to mature before drinking. If using roots these need to be cooked first until tender. Some flower and wild-plant wines require boiling water poured over them initially, or the water boiled first with the sugar before pouring over the leaves, flowers or berries. See recipes for rowan wine and elderberry wine.

Beers

These are made with malt and hops, sugar and other flavouring fermented with a little yeast. To make nettle beer use 225g (8oz or ½ peck) of young nettle tops, just under a kilo (2lb) of malt, 50g (2oz) sarsparilla, 25g (1oz) hops, 350g (12oz) loaf sugar, a little yeast and 4½l (1gall) of water. Boil nettles and malt in the water for 1 hour, then add sarsparilla, sugar and hops. Allow to cool until lukewarm, then add the yeast on toast. Leave the beer to work, bottling off before it stops. See dandelion beer page 78.

Cordials and liqueurs

These can be made at home from wild fruits and berries infused in a spirit with sugar and spices. Use brandy, whisky, gin or rum. Sloe gin is perhaps the most familiar, but you can also make blackberry or raspberry gin, strawberry brandy or cranberry whisky.

3

FRUITS AND BERRIES

Barberry (berbery, pipperidge bush)

Botanical name: *Berberis vulgaris* Family: *Berberidaceae*

Barberry is a thorny, deciduous hedgerow shrub growing from
1.8–3m (6–10ft) high. It tends to grow rather untidily, the side
branches straggling stiffly through the hedges. The tiny leaves are
sharply toothed and shiny. In late spring clusters of small, bright
yellow flowers appear which are followed by small, lozenge-shaped
berries that ripen to a brilliant red as the leaves drop in autumn. It is
fairly easy to recognise, for its thorns or spines are three-forked and
the light-coloured bark is a fierce yellow inside.

The berries are extremely sharp tasting and contain both citric
and malic acids. They are full of vitamin C and have astringent and
antiseptic properties.

Barberry grows throughout Britain but is now scarce, though it
used to be a common sight in the hedges and copses. It was eradica-
ted on a large scale when it was discovered to be the host plant of
black rust, a fungoidal disease attacking standing wheat. Gather the
bunches of berries in the autumn, from September to November,
using scissors and also wearing gloves against the thorns.

USES
Barberry berries have a sharply acid taste but with a high content of
citric acid they make an excellent amber-coloured jelly for eating
with mutton and lamb.

They can be made into jam and marmalade, or candied and used
as a garnish on sweet or savoury dishes.

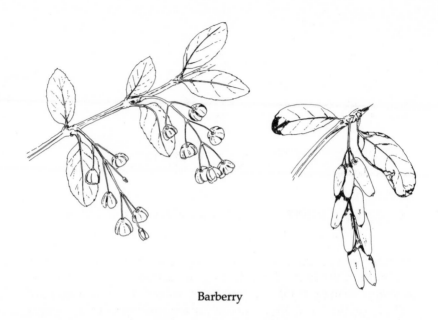

Barberry

Pickled in a strong brine with a little added alum, the berries keep their colour and can be preserved for using in the winter. Simply rinse the berries, dry them in a low oven and use to make a sauce to eat with meats.

Fresh berries can be used as a substitute for tamarind when making a curry. See also recipe for puffball, page 153.

Barberry marmalade
Into a large jar put 450g (1lb) washed berries and add 450g (1lb) preserving sugar. Stand the jar in a saucepan of boiling water until all the sugar has dissolved. Remove from heat, stir well and leave covered for 24 hours. Pour marmalade into a preserving pan and bring to the boil. Boil for 15 minutes or until set when tested on a cold plate. Pour into warm jars and seal.

Barberry preserve
Using only undamaged fruit, wash 675g (1½lb) prepared barberries and place in a heavy ovenproof pan with 275ml (10fl oz) water. Bake in a slow oven until the fruit is completely soft.

Sieve the fruit. Put pulp in a pan and add an equal weight of powdered sugar. Bring to the boil, stirring constantly. Boil for about 15 minutes until thick or until setting point is reached.

Pour into small jars and seal.

Barberry juice
Remove stalks and wash barberries. Put fruit into preserving jars and crush them a little. Add water to cover and place the lids on top. Place jars in slow oven for several hours until fruit is quite soft.

Strain through muslin allowing it to drip for an hour or two. Do not squeeze fruit. Put the juice into a pan and bring to the boil.

Pour into sterilised jars and seal.

Use in place of lemon juice for making jams and jellies and for savoury dishes.

Bilberry (whortleberry, whin, blaeberry, hurts)

Botanical name: *Vaccinium myrtillus* Family: *Ericaceae*

A low-growing shrub, bilberry is seldom seen more than 30cm (12in) high. The stiff, angular branches bear tough, leathery little leaves rather like myrtle leaves, and turn a beautiful red in autumn. The bushes spread by means of creeping underground roots. The rounded, waxy flowers are a soft red and are followed by blue-black berries which, when ripe, are covered in a greyish bloom. The berries have a slightly tart flavour when eaten raw. They are delicious when cooked and can be prepared in many different ways.

Bilberries are rich in vitamins and are very juicy. In cooking they rarely need any additional water. All edible wild fruits are more nutritious eaten raw and their unusual flavours add variety to the daily diet. Widely found on heaths and moorlands, bilberries grow throughout Britain except in the low-lying parts of southern England and East Anglia.

The berries are usually ready to pick from July onwards, though in northern parts they may not be ready until September. Make sure the berries are ripe by looking for the telltale bloom such as that found on grapes. It is a slow business gathering the berries as they grow sparsely on the low bushes and these are often hidden in the heather.

Bilberry

Fresh-picked bilberries can be eaten raw with cream and sugar. Add them to muesli for a raw fruit breakfast or cover washed berries with cold milk, leave for half an hour in the refrigerator and serve with brown sugar on a hot summer's day.

Raw bilberry juice makes a health-giving drink: Put 125g (4–5ozs) of fresh berries through the blender—you may need to add a little water—and sieve the pulp into a jug. Dilute with water and sweeten with brown sugar.

Use fresh bilberries to make pies, fruit tarts, puddings and sauces.

Gently stew bilberries to a pulp with sugar and a pinch of cinnamon.

Use to stuff pancakes.

Bilberries can be preserved by being made into jam, by bottling and by drying. Bottle them without water or syrup, allowing 50g (2oz) sugar to each pound of fruit. Put fruit and sugar into jars in layers. Fill the jars up to the top. Put the rubber rings and lids in position and fasten with clips or screwbands. Screw these up tight then unscrew a quarter turn to allow for expansion. Stand jars in pan without touching each other and cover completely with cold water. Put on the lid and heat up slowly. The water should be gently

40

simmering after one hour and this should be maintained for 15 minutes. Take jars out one at a time and tighten the screwbands immediately. Once cooled they may need further tightening. Test for sealing the following day by removing screwbands and gently lifting the bottle by its lid.

Dry bilberries by placing them between two layers of muslin on a wire cake-tray and leaving in a warm airing cupboard for 6–10 days. Store in screw-top jars. Once dried, use instead of currants in baking.

To freeze, rinse the bilberries in clean water and freeze uncovered on trays or covered with a medium or heavy syrup.

Bilberry tart

250–350g (9–12oz) berries, 50g (2oz) sugar
Wholemeal pastry: 225g (8oz) wholemeal flour, 225g (8oz) margarine, 1½ cups water, pinch salt, 1 tablespoon cream or top of the milk.

Topping: 1 dessertspoon flour, 1–2 dessertspoons sugar, ½ cup cream or milk, pinch cinnamon, 1 egg, 1 tablespoon ground almonds.

Sift flour and salt onto pastry board, cut the margarine into small pieces and work into the flour until evenly mixed. Gradually add cream and water, working it into a smooth firm paste. Roll out the pastry and line a greased baking tin. Place washed bilberries on top.

Stir ingredients for topping until a smooth mixture is obtained, pour it over the bilberries and bake in a medium oven 180° C (350° F, Gas 4) for 30–40 minutes.

Sprinkle liberally with icing sugar.

Bilberry fritters

Batter:
120g (4oz) plain flour
pinch of salt

1 egg
150ml (5fl oz) milk
fat for frying

Sieve flour and salt into a bowl. Make a well in the centre and put in the egg with half the milk. Gradually draw in the flour, mixing well. Add remaining milk and beat together until smooth and a good coating consistency. Allow to stand for ½ hour.

Add sufficient cleaned bilberries to the batter to make it really thick. Melt fat in a pan and when really hot drop in spoonfuls of batter mixture. When both sides of the fritters are golden-brown, lift out on to kitchen paper.

Serve very hot, dredged with powdered sugar.

Bilberry compote
Put 450g (1lb) well-washed bilberries into a pan with 120g (4oz) sugar and a small piece of cinnamon stick or ½ teaspoon ground cinnamon. Heat slowly until the sugar is dissolved and simmer for 5 minutes.

Mix ½ teaspoon cornflour with a little water and add to bilberries. Simmer until mixture thickens, stirring constantly.

Serve cold with rosehip macaroons (page 160)

Blackberry (bramble)

Botanical name: *Rubus fruticosus*
Rubus chamaemorus—cloudberry
Rubus caesius—dewberry
Family: *Rosaceae*

The most widely known of all the wild fruits in Britain, the blackberry is a thorny shrub which grows in untidy straggly clumps. The prickly leaves are each divided into three or more leaflets with saw-toothed edges and turn a deep red in autumn. From June to September the familiar pinky-white flowers appear looking like small single roses. These are followed by the fruits which consist of clusters of little drupes, each containing one small seed, jet black when ripe. Fully ripe fruit is very juicy and can be used in a variety of ways.

Cloudberries are blue-black when ripe, grow on short bright green stalks and look rather like bilberries. Dewberries, another member of the same family, look exactly like blackberries but the berries are smaller with fewer drupes to each cluster and they are covered with a grape-like bloom when ripe.

Blackberries contain a larger amount of vitamin A than other wild berries but less vitamin C. The berries have a high mineral content which is valuable and, in spite of the malic or citric acid in them, they leave no acid residue in the body. Blackberries can be found throughout Britain, growing in abundance in woods and clambering along the hedgerows. They grow on heaths and commons and on rough pieces of ground everywhere.

Cloudberries are mostly found growing in amongst bilberries on hills and mountain sides. Dewberries grow amongst bushes and hedges and on rough meadowland. They are mainly to be found in eastern England. From August to September the first blackberries to ripen are the lowest ones growing on each cluster. They are large, sweet and full of juice and are really best eaten raw. The remaining berries ripen later on and are less sweet and juicy but excellent for cooking.

Finally, towards October, the ripe berries have more pip than pulp and should be used in blackberry-and-apple dishes or for making bramble jelly. October berries are considered 'sour and sodden' and jam made with them will not set.

USES

Eat raw the first blackberries of the season. Wash them lightly if necessary and serve with cream and a sprinkle of chopped hazelnuts. Add them to fresh fruit salad or use to decorate a cold lemon soufflé or a light sponge cake being served as a sweet.

If the fruit is mushy make it into raw juice by putting it into an electric blender then through a sieve. Keep it in a jar in the refrigerator. Dilute the juice with water and sweeten with brown sugar for a refreshing drink.

Use the second picking of blackberries to make pies and tarts, adding a knob of butter and a pinch of cinnamon, or mix them with a little stewed apple.

Lightly cook blackberries with other soft fruits to make a fruit fool, or use them on their own.

For blackberry pudding mix double the amount of blackberries to chopped dessert apples sweetened with honey. Line a bowl with slices of bread and butter and pour in the fruit mixture. Cover with more bread and butter and steam for 1–2 hours. Eat cold with thin cream.

Blackberry sauce is very good with ice cream or a plain steamed sponge pudding. Blackberry-leaf tea is made from the tips of the young leaves. These can be fresh or dried for the purpose and the tea is taken as a tonic.

Blackberries can be preserved for winter use made into jams, jellies, ketchup, cordials or wine. They are successful when bottled whole, pulped or as juice, and pickled blackberries are tasty when eaten with cold meats. For freezing choose the really ripe fruit and remove the stems and leaves. Rinse quickly in cold water and drain on kitchen paper. Freeze in medium syrup or use dry sugar—120g (4oz) to 450g (1lb) fruit. Alternatively spread the berries on a large plate or plastic tray and freeze uncovered until hard. Remove from trays and put them into one large polythene bag. As they do not stick together frozen in this way you can use a small quantity at a time.

Blackberry cheese
Make only a small quantity at a time though it will keep for up to two months in the refrigerator or if airtight.

450g (1lb) juicy blackberries	1 lemon
225g (8oz) sugar	2 eggs
1 cooking apple finely chopped	120g (4oz) butter

Put blackberries and apple in a pan over low heat. Stir and crush the fruit with a wooden spoon until soft. Put fruit through a blender to make a smooth pulp and remove seeds by sieving. Mix together the pulp, sugar, butter, juice and grated rind of lemon and the eggs well beaten and pour into a double saucepan. Stir until the mixture becomes thick. Pot and seal.

Blackberry pudding

225g (8oz) flour	150ml (5fl oz) milk
pinch salt	450g (1lb) ripe blackberries
3 teaspoons baking powder	25g (1oz) sugar
50g (2oz) margarine	pinch cinnamon

Sieve flour, salt and baking powder together. Rub in margarine until it resembles breadcrumbs. Add milk to make a soft dough. Turn onto a floured board and knead until smooth. Roll out pastry to ½inch thick. Cover with blackberries, sprinkle with sugar and cinnamon. Roll up pastry and place on baking tin, seam side downwards.
Bake in a hot oven, 200°C (400°F, Gas 6), for 25–30 minutes.

Blackberry cordial
Make this when there are plenty of blackberries about. Add 900g

(2lb) sugar to 2¼l (4pt) strained blackberry juice. Bring to the boil and lightly skim. Add 12g (½oz) each of cloves and cinnamon and 20g (¾oz) nutmeg. Bring to the boil and simmer until the cordial is rich and spicy. Cool, then add 275ml (10fl oz) brandy and pour into bottles.

Dilute with soda water.

Bullace

Botanical name: *Prunus insititia* Family: *Rosaceae*

The bullace tree is regarded by some authorities as the origin of all the plums, and it grows abundantly throughout Britain in hedges and open woods. It can grow to 6m (20ft) high and many of its smaller branches end in a thorn. The leaves are downy, oval and finely toothed. Small white flowers appear in early spring before the leaves. The fruits are globular and vary in colour from yellow to black and when ripe have a soft grape-like bloom to them. The yellow bullace is often called the white damson.

Bullace plums are small and very astringent with a strong but not unpleasant acid taste. They contain vitamin A. They can be

Bullace

gathered when ripe in late autumn, and the best time is after they have had a frost on them.

USES

Much of the flavour of the bullace plum lies in the kernel. Long, slow cooking will help to extract the flavour and juice and this is delicious when added to elderberry or bilberry recipes.

Add bullace plums to marrow when making jam and to apples in pies and puddings.

Bullace gin is made by pricking 450g (1lb) clean ripe bullaces with a needle, putting them into a jar with half their weight in sugar and covering with a bottle of gin. Keep it airtight. It can be used within two months if sufficient flavour has developed.

Bullaces can be made into jelly or chutney to serve with meat dishes as well as a marmalade to eat at breakfast.

Other uses for the bullace are the same as for plums, though more sugar will always be required.

Bullaces can be frozen but are best when bottled in a medium syrup. As the fruits are so small there is a high proportion of stones to flesh. To get over this problem make them into a purée and keep in screwtop jars.

Bullace chutney

450g (1lb) bullace plums
1 cooking apple, peeled, cored and chopped
1 large onion peeled and chopped
75g (3oz) sultanas
350g (12oz) sugar

425ml (¾pt) vinegar
6g (¼oz) each cloves and ginger
½ dried red chilli
1 teaspoon salt
pinch dry mustard

Cook bullaces gently until soft but still whole. Drain and remove the stones. Put in a pan with all other ingredients except the sugar, tying up the spices in a muslin bag. Add vinegar and simmer gently for 20–30 minutes. Add sugar and boil until thick. Pot and seal.

Bullace jam

900g (2lb) bullaces
900g (2lb) sugar

Use only whole undamaged bullaces and wipe or wash fruit if

necessary. Put bullaces in a pan with sugar and a little water to prevent burning. Slowly bring to the boil, stirring occasionally, until sugar is dissolved. Boil hard for 10 minutes or until setting point is reached. Remove stones.

Pour into warmed jars and seal.

Bullace gin
450g (1lb) bullaces   225g (½lb) sugar
1 bottle gin

Use whole unbruised fruit. Prick each bullace once or twice with a skewer. Tip them into a large jar and add the sugar. Pour gin on top. Seal and leave for six weeks before using.

Cherry plum

Botanical name: *Prunus cerasifera*
Prunus cerasus—wild cherry
Prunus avium—gean
Family: *Rosaceae*

The cherry plum closely resembles the blackthorn in appearance, but it is not so thickset and the glossy green twigs are thornless and turn a reddish-brown as the season develops. It grows to the size of a small tree, 4½–6m (15–20ft), and early in spring loose spikes of white flowers appear at the same time as the pale green shiny leaves. The fruits which follow are round and a mixture of red and yellow, but they do not form every year.

The wild cherry is a shrub, growing about 1½–2½m (5–8ft), which throws up numerous suckers from creeping roots. The flowers are white and appear before the leaves, and the fruit is round, smooth and has no bloom on it. The colour of the fruit is either deep red or black and it resembles the cultivated morello cherry.

The gean is the tree variety of the wild cherry, growing up to 18m (60ft). The drooping, copper-coloured leaves are downy beneath and turn pink in autumn. The bark is smooth, shiny and reddish-brown. Large clusters of white, rose-like flowers which bloom in April and May are followed by round, red fruits which can be either sweet or bitter.

The fruit of all three species can be eaten but is very acid and needs to be cooked first with plenty of sugar. They are mildly laxative. The cherry plum and wild cherry can be found growing in woods and hedgerows throughout England and Wales and in southern Scotland, but the cherry plum is less common. The gean tree grows in hedges and beech woods in the southern half of the British Isles. Gather all cherries when ripe, from August onwards.

USES

Cherries keep well either bottled or frozen in a heavy syrup (see bilberry, page 41). Later, use them for pies and tarts.

Any that are bitter are best made into jelly or used for cherry brandy.

Cherry plum jam
Pick only very ripe cherries and remove the stones. An easy way to do this is by pushing a small hairpin into the stalk opening, twisting it round the stone, then giving a sharp pull. Put cherries into a pan with water to cover, and boil gently until soft. Add an equal weight of sugar, together with red currant or apple juice as pectin in the proportion 150ml (5fl oz) to 900g (2lb) pulp. Dissolve the sugar, then boil hard for 10 minutes or until set when tested on a cold plate.

Pot and seal.

Cherry plum sauce

450g (1lb) red currant jelly	450g (1lb) sugar
900g (2lb) ripe cherry plums	2 tablespoons brandy

Melt the red currant jelly slowly over gentle heat. Stone the plums and add them to the melted jelly. Set aside to cool.

Serve with raspberry water ice, recipe page 60.

Cherry plum compote
Put ripe cherry plums into a pan with just enough red wine to cover. Add some sugar to taste and a pinch of cinnamon. Bring the mixture slowly to the boil. Simmer very gently for 10 minutes. Strain off the cherries, return syrup to pan and add a tablespoon of red currant jelly to each 450g (1lb) fruit.

Serve chilled, with thin cream.

Crab apple

Botanical name: *Malus sylvestris* or *Pyrus malus* Family: *Rosaceae*

Sometimes difficult to pick out in the wild state, the crab apple is a species from which the ordinary garden apples are descended. It is a small, very spiny, deciduous tree with reddish-brown twigs and little, oval-shaped leaves, short-stalked and downy. The pinky-white flowers grow in clusters and bloom in May.

The fruits which follow are tart and a yellowish-green colour which later often turns to scarlet. They are much smaller and more acid than the ordinary apple. Some crab apples have thorns and small, very sour fruit, whilst others are pleasanter to eat. Many of the wild trees will be recognised as 'escapes', perhaps from apple orchards nearby.

Crab apples are highly astringent and contain vitamins A and C. Wild crab apples grow in the woods and amongst the dense hedgerows of the countryside and are widespread throughout Britain. The crab apple season is usually October but they are not ready to be gathered until touched by frost which cuts the acid taste considerably.

USES

Crab apples are too tart to eat raw, but cooked can be used in a variety of ways. The best crab apple jelly is made from the sourest of the crab apple crop and the attractive pale pink or deep red jelly is good with cold meats.

After cooking the crab apples and draining off the juice for jelly making, sieve the remaining pulp and mix it with sugar. Use this purée in puddings and pies, or make into a sauce to serve with shellfish.

Mix crab apple jelly with cooked fruits such as blackberries or elderberries for an open-tart filling.

Verjuice, more tart than lemon juice, is made from crab apples and is useful in some recipes. Chop up fully ripened crab apples roughly and put through a juice extractor. Store the juice in a screw-top bottle. Crab apples can be frozen using fully ripe fruit. Remove the stalks and wipe over each apple with a damp cloth before freezing.

To preserve crab apples, wash and dry perfect fruit and leave the stalks on. Prick them all over with a needle. Make a heavy syrup using 450g (1lb) sugar to 275ml (10fl oz) water. When syrup is clear add the apples, which must be covered by the syrup, the juice of a lemon and a piece of ginger. Simmer gently until apples are tender but still whole. Remove the ginger. Bottle and seal.

Crab apple conserve

An unusual preserve to eat at breakfast. Choose large ripe crab apples, peel and core, then cut each one into thin slices. Place them in a pan with a little water. Bring slowly to the boil and simmer gently until the fruit is soft and mushy, stirring frequently. Sieve the fruit and weigh the pulp. Return pulp to pan and add equal weight of sugar. Stir until dissolved then boil it gently for 10 minutes, stirring nearly all the time.

Pot and seal.

Crab apple jelly

Wash crabs and cut them into quarters without peeling or coring. Put into a pan, cover with cold water and boil to a pulp.

Strain through a jelly bag and measure the juice. Allow 450g (1lb) sugar to 575ml (1pt) juice and stir until the sugar is dissolved, then boil hard until setting point is reached.

Pot and seal in the usual way.

Cranberry

Botanical name: *Vaccinium oxycoccus* Family: *Ericaceae*

Cranberry is a plant of peat bogs and wet heather throughout Britain, but is no longer as plentiful as it used to be because of the systematic drainage and reclamation of wastelands. It is nowadays more or less confined to the north-west. It is a low, evergreen shrub with a creeping rootstock. The leaves are small and arrow-shaped with their edges turned back. Bright pink flowers droop down on long stalks and bloom during June and July. The small, round, red-spotted fruits ripen in the autumn.

Full of mineral salts, cranberries used to be considered valuable in cases of anaemia, though they are too acid to be eaten raw. Gather them when fully ripe in the autumn.

Cranberries cooked until tender and beaten with sugar become the well-known sauce served with roast turkey.

Raw cranberry juice has a good flavour and can be added to apple or blackberry dishes in place of lemon juice. Add semolina or corn-flour to thicken it.

Cranberry cheese is delicious served with cold poultry, pork or veal. Cranberry cordial is a healthy warming drink. The berries can also be made into jam, alone or combined with apple. When making jelly, a few drops of colouring may be added.

For a tart, use cooked, mashed cranberries and fill the pastry when they are cold.

Berries can be used to make a spicy ketchup to eat with chicken rissoles.

Cranberry shape to eat with green salads
Put washed cranberries into a saucepan with a little water and simmer until soft. Add sugar and beat together until well mixed and sugar dissolved. Soften sufficient gelatine to set the cranberries to a firm jelly. Leave to set. Chop into pieces and sprinkle over the salad.

Cranberry spiced sauce

900g (2lb) cranberries	1 teaspoon mixed spice
275ml (½pt) water	6 whole cloves
175g (6oz) brown sugar	12 whole allspice
2 teaspoons lemon juice	

In a pan put washed fruit, water and the spices tied in muslin. Bring to the boil and simmer until soft.

Remove spices and press pulp through a sieve or use a blender. Return pulp to pan together with the sugar. Stir until sugar is dis-solved then simmer for 2 minutes.

Leave to cool and pot in the usual way.

Use with meats and poultry.

Cranberry steamed pudding

225g (8oz) cranberries	3 eggs
120g (4oz) sugar	½ teaspoon cinnamon
120g (4oz) butter	2 teaspoons grated rind of an orange
120g (4oz) breadcrumbs	150ml (5fl oz) milk

Mix butter and sugar together until soft and creamy. Add sugar and beat until smooth. Beat eggs and add. Mix cinnamon with breadcrumbs and add to mixture. Add orange rind and milk and mix well. Lastly fold in the cranberries.

Mix together well and pour into a buttered basin. Cover and steam for 3 hours.

Serve with brandy sauce or a creamy custard.

Elder

Botanical name: *Sambucus nigra* Family: *Caprifoliaceae*

A familiar, fast-growing shrub or small tree, the common elder has large pointed leaves made up of five to seven leaflets with a sharp unpleasant smell when young. The stems and branches are full of white pith and the young twigs are covered in scales. The flowers, of tiny, creamy-white blossoms, are particularly fragrant and grow in large, flat-topped clusters, appearing in early summer. The shiny black berries which follow are full of juice.

Elderberries are rich in mineral salts and, though mainly used in cooking, have medicinal properties. Elder is a common plant and can be found growing in woods, copses, hedgerows and waste land throughout the British Isles. Birds are fond of the berries and carry the seeds far and wide. Gather the clusters of berries in early autumn when they are soft, jet-black and hanging downwards.

USES

Elderberries are delicious stewed with a pinch of mixed spice or cinnamon. Mix with apples, using twice as much apple to elderberries, and add chopped lemon balm and sugar. To make elderberry syrup, wash and drain the berries, with stalks removed. Put berries in a pan, cover liberally with water and boil for 10 minutes. Strain through muslin cloth. Add 350g (12oz) sugar to 575ml (1pt) juice and boil for 10–15 minutes. Remove from heat, skim, pour into warm bottles and seal. Use the syrup in sauces and fruit fools, or make a mulled drink in winter with brandy and cinnamon.

Use elderberries in pies and tarts and for a tasty ketchup. Make elderberry wine or jam or a jelly mixed with crab apples for an unusual flavour.

Preserve elderberries by drying (see bilberry, p 41), by freezing on their own or in medium syrup, or by potting them: to do this, place the berries in a large stone jar between layers of sugar until the jar is full. Cover closely and leave in a slow oven until juice is flowing freely. Remove from the oven and seal the jar whilst hot.

Elderflowers picked just as the tiny flowers are opening make an unusual-flavoured syrup or cordial to add to fruit salads or to take as a cooling drink diluted with soda water.

For elderflower fritters, dip flowerheads, lightly washed, into a thick batter and plunge them into deep fat until the fritter is golden. Serve them with a dusting of icing sugar.

Elderflower pickle
Pick elderflowers on a dry day and just as the flowers begin to open. Cut off any stems, pack the flowers into small jars and cover them with boiling white wine vinegar. Cover the jars and leave for several weeks. Serve with cold meats and green salad.

Elderberry ketchup
Strip berries from stalks, wash and drain. Place in a pan and cover with an equal quantity of wine vinegar and cider. Add a small clove of garlic, sprig of thyme, a little fennel and a bay leaf. Bring to the boil and simmer very slowly for 2 hours. Strain, then add pinch of salt and a little sugar. Bring to the boil, remove from the heat, add a few peppercorns, then bottle and seal.

Spiced elderberry wine

2 kg (4½lb) elderberries	4½l (1gall) water
1½ kg (3¼lb) demerara sugar	225g (8oz) raisins, chopped
6g (¼oz) whole cloves (about 6)	12g (½oz) root ginger, bruised
1 small stick cinnamon	1 lemon, sliced
1 teaspoon wine yeast	

Mash the stripped elderberries in a large bowl and pour over the gallon of boiling water. Leave for two days stirring daily, then strain through a jelly bag into a large pan.

Put the lemon, ginger, cinnamon and cloves into a muslin bag and boil it in a pint (575ml) of the juice for 20 minutes. Remove the bag and when the juice is cool add it to the juice in the pan. Dissolve the sugar in the juice, add the creamed yeast and raisins.

Pour into clean storage jars, keeping any surplus in a bottle for topping up after fermentation has stopped.

Place jars on a tray to catch the froth and when this has stopped, clean up the jars and fit them with airlocks or loose-fitting corks. When gas bubbles no longer form, rack or syphon off the wine into second storage jars, filling to the top. Insert corks, waxing the tops, and store jars in a cool place for at least six months, then syphon off again into clean bottles and cork down.

Store bottles on their sides for a further six months.

For an unspiced wine, use the same quantities of fruit, water and yeast. Pour the boiling water over the crushed fruit and allow to cool before adding the yeast. Leave for three days stirring daily. Strain through jelly bag, dissolve 1½ kg (3¼lb) white sugar in the juice and then proceed as for the spiced wine.

Elderberry fool

450g (1lb) elderberries	275ml (10fl oz) milk
75g (3oz) sugar	25g (1oz) custard powder

Cook the berries in very little water until soft and mushy. Rub through sieve and sweeten to taste. Blend custard powder with a little milk and bring remaining milk to the boil. Pour on to custard powder stirring well.

Return mixture to pan and cook until thick, stirring constantly.

Mix it with the fruit purée and serve cold.

Potted elderberries

450g (1lb) elderberries	50g (2oz) sugar

Put a layer of washed berries in a jar and sprinkle with sugar. Continue layers until jar is full, then cover. Stand jar in pan of simmering water until juice has flowed. Remove jar and seal whilst hot.

Use to make sauce for ice cream and as a base for other recipes.

Hawthorn (may, whitethorn)

Botanical name: *Crataegus oxyacantha* Family: *Rosaceae*

A thorny prolific shrub or small tree, common hawthorn has sweet-smelling flowers which bloom in spring or early summer. The

Hawthorn—flowers and 'haws'

leaves are divided into three or five segments and can vary considerably, being either sharply toothed or roundly lobed. Flowers are small with broad white or pink petals and grow in corymbs. The variety *Crataegus monogyna* is known as quickthorn. It has white flowers and more deeply cut leaves.

The fruits or 'haws' are crimson-red and have two or three seeds in each berry. They have little juice and are somewhat mealy in texture but have a sweet taste. Hawthorns are widespread throughout the British Isles in woods, hedgerows and copses. They are also widely cultivated as hedges. The best time to pick the fruit is in September and October when it is a vivid red and fully ripe.

USES

Use 'haws' to make hawthorn jelly to eat with meats or cream cheese.

Or open the haws to remove the seeds, dry these and use them in place of coffee.

Hawthorn jelly
To every 450g (1lb) fruit add 275ml (10fl oz) water. Bring to the boil and simmer gently until soft. Strain through a muslin cloth overnight. Measure juice, then add 450g (1lb) sugar to every 575ml (1pt) of juice. Heat to dissolve sugar, then boil hard for 10 minutes or until jelly sets when tested on a cold plate. Pot and when cold, cover and seal.

Hawthorn berry wine
Put ripe haws into a pan and pour boiling water over them, 575ml (20fl oz) water to 450g (1lb) fruit. Leave to stand for six weeks.

Then remove the crust that forms on top. Strain the liquid through muslin and add 450g (1lb) sugar to every 575ml (20fl oz) of liquid. Pour into a jar, fill to the top, and when fermentation has finished, bottle and leave for as long as possible before drinking.

Juniper

Botanical name: *Juniperus communis* Family: *Pinaceae*

A sweet, strongly aromatic shrub, the common juniper is a sturdy, much-branched evergreen. The bushes can grow up to 4.6m (15ft) high or they may be low-growing and rather flat. The needle-like leaves are sharp and prickly. The greenish flowers are small catkins. The berries are round and turn a dark, purplish-blue when fully ripe, with a whitish bloom all over them. Pea-sized, they take three years to ripen. They have a mealy texture and a sweet, spicy taste which gives gin its characteristic flavour.

Juniper berries are antiseptic and contain substances which stimulate the appetite and are good for the digestion. Juniper bushes can be found growing on hills and chalk downs in the British Isles, but are most common in the north. A few ripe berries can be found at all times of the year, but September and October are the usual months for gathering.

USES
Juniper berries can be used freshly picked from the bushes, but are more usually dried. Used mostly as a spice in marinades for game and meats, three or four berries can replace a bay leaf.

56

Make juniper syrup and take a teaspoon before meals to increase the appetite.

For a very good savoury spice, add crushed juniper berries to boiling bacon and creamed cabbage. Use in pickling spices for hams, chutneys and pickles.

Juniper preserve

Cook berries in water to cover, simmering gently until they are soft. Put into a blender and then through a sieve to get a smooth pulp. Add 350g (12oz) of sugar to 120g (4oz) pulp whilst warm. Beat together until sugar is dissolved and the mixture is thick, put into small jars and seal. Eat with roast duck or pheasant.

Pickled white cabbage with junipers

Take off outer leaves of a medium-sized cabbage and cut into quarters, cutting out the stalk. Wash thoroughly and shred it finely. Pile the cabbage into a large bowl or onto a dish, and sprinkle liberally with salt, adding 5–6 crushed juniper berries. Leave to stand for 24 hours.

Drain and pack into jars. Fill the jars with cold well-flavoured stock and seal in the usual way.

Juniper marinade

275ml (10fl oz) red wine
150ml (5fl oz) oil
1 small onion, chopped small
2 tablespoons lemon juice
small clove garlic, crushed

4 whole cloves
6 juniper berries, crushed
salt
1 bay leaf

Mix all the ingredients together in a bowl and leave to stand, covered, overnight.

Use to marinate poultry or game for 24 hours.

Medlar

Botanical name: *Mespilus germanica* Family: *Rosaceae*

The common medlar is a thorny shrub or small tree growing to 4½m (15ft). The long, oval leaves are slightly toothed and usually downy on the undersides. The large single flowers are white with touches of pink and bloom in spring. The large, brown, fleshy fruit is hard and almost round with a distinctive hairy disc on top. It has a pleasant, sweet flavour. Medlar trees can be found growing wild in southern England. The fruits should be gathered in the autumn.

USES
Medlars can be used fresh when they are split open and the brown flesh eaten with cream and brown sugar.

Traditionally in England medlars are picked and 'bletted'—left to get soft for a week or two—before being eaten. The taste develops this way but they look less attractive to eat.

Medlars make an excellent jelly which tastes exactly like guava jelly and is good with cold meats.

Baked medlars
Choose firm, ripe medlars, remove the hairy disc and wipe them. Place them in a shallow dish with enough water to cover the bottom. Dot generously with butter and add a few cloves or piece of cinnamon. Bake in a moderate oven 170°C (325°F, Gas 3) for 20–30 minutes. Serve with cream and sugar.

Medlar cheese
Put cleaned medlars into a pan with 150ml (5fl oz) water to every

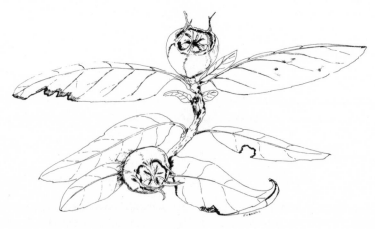

Medlar

58

Dog rose—flower and hips

spread throughout the British Isles, growing on waste land, in hedgerows and fields. The hips which grow in Scotland contain much more vitamin C than those growing further south.

Rosehips for cooking should be gathered late in autumn when fully ripe and after being touched by frost, when they will be slightly soft. Rosehips for drying should be picked when fully ripe but firm.

USES

Use rosehips in cooking to make purée, puddings, ice cream, syrups and sauces.

Rosehips can be preserved by freezing quite successfully, but should not be left too long in the freezer. The hips can also be dried by cutting them in half and spreading them on a wire tray, leaving them in a very low oven, or the airing cupboard, until dried but still red. Once dry, rub the hips over a hair sieve to remove the tiny hairs which can cause irritation if swallowed.

61

Rosehip purée, made with fresh hips
Top and tail ripe hips, wash quickly and drain, then put them in a saucepan and cover with boiling water. Simmer with lid on for about 15 minutes. Purée the softened hips by sieving or milling.

Beat in to the purée an equal quantity of fine sugar and boil gently for 10 minutes.

This purée can also be made with dried hips, and will keep for a long time in sealed airtight jars stored in a cool dark cupboard.

Rosehip syrup keeps well in stoppered jars and can be used diluted with water for a healthy refreshing drink or added to fruit salads and soft-fruit puddings.

Sweet rosehip sauce
Take 75–100g (3–4oz) fresh rosehip purée and simmer gently with 275ml (10fl oz) apple juice, a pinch of cinnamon and sugar to taste. Use hot over ice cream or with a sponge pudding.

Rosehip tart
Wash rosehips, cut in half and remove the seeds. Cover with water and cook gently to a pulp. Rub through a sieve. Add a pinch of cinnamon, a little lemon and icing sugar to taste. Roll out shortcrust pastry very thinly, line a pie plate, fill with rosehips and cover with more pastry. Cook in a moderate oven for 30 minutes or until pastry is golden-brown. Dust the top with icing sugar and serve hot or cold.

Rosehip ice cream
In an electric mixer beat together 1 egg and 150ml (¼pt) double cream. Gradually add 120g (4oz) sugar and 275ml (½pt) rosehip purée. Lastly add a pinch of salt and 425ml (15fl oz) milk. Beat until quite smooth. Pour into a tray and freeze until firm, about 4 hours.

Rosehip conserve
Gather fully ripe red rosehips, cut open and scrape out the seeds. Put into a bowl and pour boiling water over them. Leave to stand until soft, then rub through a sieve or use an electric blender.

Mix the pulp with its equal weight of fine sugar, put into small pots and cover.

Rosehip soup
Wash and chop roughly 225g (8oz) rosehips. Put into a pan with
850ml (1½pt) water, and sugar to taste. Add a pinch of cinnamon
and simmer till soft.
Sieve the fruit and thicken the soup if necessary with 25g (1oz)
cornflour.
Serve with plain boiled rice.

Rosehip macaroons see under Almonds, page 160.

Rowan (Mountain Ash)

Botanical name: *Sorbus aucuparia*
Sorbus torminalis—wild service tree
Sorbus latifolia—french hales
Sorbus aria—whitebeam
Family: *Rosaceae*

The rowan tree is a familiar sight in the countryside. Easy to recognise with its pinnate leaves, the eleven to nineteen leaflets so regu-
larly paired with a single one at the end. The leaflets are long,
narrow and evenly toothed. The creamy-white flowers are small but
grow in profuse bunches and bloom in spring or early summer. The
numerous berries which follow are small, round and light red.
The wild service tree is more of a tall shrub. The broad leaves are
divided into pointed lobes. The white flowers grow in corymbs but
are larger than those of the rowan and there are fewer of them. The
fruits are small, egg-shaped and brown.
French hales is a locally found species of sorbus. The leaves are
larger and have more triangular lobes than the whitebeam, with a
grey down on the undersides. The berries vary from orange to
brown.
The whitebeam is a handsome tree or tall bush with toothed, oval
leaves, silvery-green and very downy underneath. The small, white
flowers grow in less profusion than the rowan but are similarly
followed by dull red berries.
The rowan grows throughout the British Isles, but is more commonly found in the north and west in woods and rocky places sometimes high up in the mountains. The wild service tree grows on clay
or limestone soils in England and Wales. French hales grow in

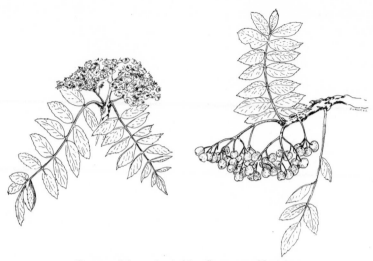

Rowan (Moutain Ash)—flower and berries

woods and hedges only in south-west England. Whitebeam is more common and grows in woods all over the British Isles but is more frequent in England on chalk or limestone.

The berries are ripe and ready to be gathered from early August.

USES

The fruits of the rowan and other sorbus are very astringent and have a slightly bitter taste, but make an attractive orange-red jelly to eat with venison and hare. They combine well with other fruits such as apple or crab apple. Make jelly as page 33, but first soak the berries in hot water to remove some of the tartness.

Rowan wine

Pick dry rowan berries when fully ripe and put them in a bowl. Mash them down, then cover with boiling water. Cover the whole with a cloth and leave for three days. Drain and measure the juice. To each 4½l (1gall) of juice add 450g (1lb) sugar and stir till dissolved. Pour into brown stone jars, making sure they are full.

Cover lightly and leave to work for one week. Fasten tightly when working has finished and leave for six months.

Pour into stoppered bottles.

Rowan pudding
725ml (1¼pt) rowan berry juice   50g (2oz) semolina
275ml (10fl oz) water   1 dessertspoon cornflour
120g (4oz) sugar

Put rowans into a pan and cover with water and a lid. Bring quickly to the boil then boil gently until soft.

Strain through a jelly bag. Measure the required amount of rowan juice and put in a pan with the water. Bring to the boil, add sugar, stir in semolina and boil about 10 minutes. Mix cornflour with a little water, add to the mixture and reboil.

Pour into a pudding mould and leave to get quite cold.

Turn out and serve with thin cream or custard.

Rowan Kissel
This dish is made in exactly the same way as the pudding, but the rowan juice and sugar are boiled together to make a syrup before being thickened with cornflour.

Serve cold, in a glass bowl, decorated with whipped cream.

Sloe *(Blackthorn)*

Botanical name: *Prunus spinosa* Family: *Rosaceae*

Blackthorn is a tough, thorny, hedge shrub with long, finely toothed oval leaves, and the small white flowers appear before the leaves, alone or in pairs. The fruits, the sloes, are small, round and almost black, covered with a soft bloom. These are rather dry and bitter and are rarely eaten raw. The berries are very astringent and acid.

Blackthorn bushes are common throughout the British Isles, but they produce better crops of sloes in the southern half of the country. They grow along hedges and roadsides, in woods and on open, grassy waste land. The time to gather the sloes is towards the end of October when they are fully ripe and at their best.

USES
Sloe gin is a well-known drink; after making it keep the sloes in an airtight jar to use in an apple pie. Sloes can be used to make a wine

which, if left for 12 months, is an excellent drink (see below).

Make jelly using sloes on their own or mixed with apples or crab apples. Or stew sloes slowly to extract the juice and combine with bilberries or elderberries to make a good cornflour mould.

Sloe and apple pudding

Stand 675g (1½lb) sloes in a jar and fill up with water. Stand the jar in a saucepan of cold water and bring to the boil. Cook 1½kg (3lb) apples and stew to a pulp in very little water; put pulp through blender and then a sieve. Mix sloe juice and apple pulp together and add 225g (½lb) sugar to each 450g (1lb) of fruit. Boil for 30–40 minutes or until mixture sets. Pour into small jelly moulds.

When cold, turn out and serve with cream.

Sloe wine

Gather sufficient sloes to fill a one litre (nearly 2pt) jug. Prick each with a needle and put into a jar. Pour over 1 litre (2pt) boiling water. When cooled, crush sloes with wooden spoon or masher. Leave to stand for 3 days.

Strain and add 900g (2lb) sugar and half a thinly sliced lemon. Stir occasionally till sugar is melted. Pour into a wine jar and leave lightly corked for a few days, then fasten down tightly.

Sloe wine is at its best if left for a year.

Strawberry

Botanical name: *Fragaria vesca* Family: *Rosaceae*

The small, sweetly aromatic fruit of the wild strawberry is one of the most delicious of all wild fruits. Very easy to recognise, it looks like a smaller edition of the cultivated strawberry. The plants spread fairly rapidly by means of runners which then put down roots.

The little white flowers start blooming in early spring and continue for three months. The red berries which follow are not really fruits but enlarged fruit axes and bear the tiny fruitlets on the surface.

Wild strawberries are highly nutritious, containing vitamins and mineral salts. They are common in woods, copses and under hedges throughout Britain, mainly on chalky soils.

There are countless uses for wild strawberries, but for flavour they are best eaten soon after picking with a little sugar and cream.

For a sumptuous dish, put strawberries into a deep plate, smother them with icing sugar and pour champagne over the top.

Use fresh berries for ice creams, summer puddings and cooling drinks.

The berries can be preserved in jams or jellies, by bottling or freezing. Bottled strawberries are rather disappointing as they shrink and discolour.

Freezing, either plain or in a heavy syrup, is successful, but the berries are flabby if thawed out too quickly. However preserved, strawberries are good used in sweet omelettes, fruit salads, jellies, sauces and fruit tarts.

Wild strawberry cup
Cut in half 450g (1lb) fresh wild strawberries. Put in a bowl with 150g (5oz) sifted sugar and leave to stand for an hour. Stir, then pour onto them 1.1l (2pt) apple juice and 275ml (½pt) soda water.

Chill in refrigerator before serving.

Wild strawberry preserve (uncooked)
Stir equal weights of fresh wild strawberries and sugar in a bowl for about ½ hour. Pot up. Seal carefully and store in a cool place.

This raw preserve does not keep as long as cooked jams.

Strawberry Bowl
1 bottle light white wine   50g (2oz) sugar
120g–175g (4–6oz) strawberries

Cover strawberries with sugar and pour over half the bottle of wine. Cover and leave for half an hour or longer, then add remaining wine.

Serve chilled with a dash of soda water.

Quick strawberry mousse
Mash 450g (1lb) strawberries with a little lemon juice and add sugar to taste. Fold in 275ml (10fl oz) whipped cream and put into individual glass dishes. Serve chilled with wafer biscuits.

4

LEAVES, STEMS AND ROOTS

Alexanders (black lovage, black potherb)

Botanical name: *Smyrnium olusatrum* Family: *Umbelliferae*

A tall, hairless biennial, alexanders has numerous heads of greenish-yellow flower umbels which appear in April and June. The toothed, glossy leaves grow in groups of three on a thick sheath attached to the solid, furrowed stem.

The fruits are black when fully ripe and the whole plant has a pungent celery-like aroma.

Alexanders grows abundantly on waste ground and hedge banks, often within a few miles of the coast. Sometimes the leaves appear as early as January and these are best collected when young, but edible stalks and stems are gathered later in the season when they are a reasonable size. Alexanders is somewhat similar to wild angelica (*Angelica sylvestris*) which has pinky-white flowers, and to wild celery (*Apium graveolens*) with white flowers; both are edible.

USES

The spicy leaves of alexanders are good in salads or sandwiches, cooked as a green vegetable or as flavouring in soups and stews.

Try the flower buds dipped in batter and deep fried until golden-brown. Serve hot with fresh tomato sauce and a green salad.

The best part of the plant to eat is the stem, prepared and cooked like celery.

Alexanders stems
Take off the long leaf stems near the base of the plant; this is the

pinkish tender part. Peel and cut into short lengths. Cook in lightly salted water for 10 minutes. Serve with melted butter mixed with two tablespoons of crisp breadcrumbs.

Brooklime

Botanical name: *Veronica beccabunga* Family: *Scrophulariaceae*

A low, creeping, rather straggling perennial, brooklime grows like watercress. The smooth fleshy leaves are oval-shaped and slightly toothed. From May to September small, bright-blue flowers grow on stalked spikes at the bases of the upper leaves. It is commonly found in wet places throughout Britain.

Brooklime is a valuable winter salad plant which is anti-scorbutic and contains vitamin C, tannin, a bitter principle, volatile oil and a little sulphur. These constituents produce its bitter flavour.

Brooklime

69

Gather brooklime as soon as it appears, which can be as early as February, and before it flowers.

Full of health-giving properties, brooklime leaves can be used raw in salads, a little at a time because of their strong flavour. The leaves and stems also make a good vegetable cooked like spinach.

Brooklime spring drink
In spring, express the juice of a handful of young brooklime leaves and mix with an equal quantity of juice from Seville oranges. Sweeten with honey and take a small drink each day.

Bulrush (reedmace, cat's tail)

> Botanical name: *Typha latifolia*
> *Typha angustifolia*—lesser reedmace
> Family: *Typhaceae*

This food plant should not be confused with the true bulrush (*Scirpus lacustris*) which is a tall feathery grass-like rush. The reedmace is a tall perennial with long, sword-like, flat leaves. The stout stem, between 1.8m (6ft) and 2m (7ft) tall, is topped by the 'mace', a brown, tube-shaped spike of female flowers with an upper, narrower spear of fluffy yellow male flowers. After flowering the 'mace' becomes bare and wispy, while the lower part carries the developing seeds surrounded by brown cottony hairs.

The lesser reedmace is similar in appearance but smaller. The male and female flower spikes are separated by a short length of stalk.

The bulrush is common throughout Britain beside ponds, lakes, reedy swamps and along most waterways, though it is rare in Scotland. The lesser reedmace is scarcer and quite difficult to find.

USES
All edible parts of the reedmace plants have a sweet taste. Peel young stems carefully and cook the white, inner part in boiling water until tender. Eat like asparagus, dipping the stems into melted, herb-flavoured butter.

Peel and cook the young roots as a vegetable or grate them raw into a salad.

Bulrush

The seeds can also be eaten and have a pleasant nutty taste when roasted. They are well worth the lengthy job of extracting them from the fluffy hairs.

In times of shortage, bulrush pollen can be used as a flour substitute.

Bulrush-stem salad
Wash and peel young bulrush shoots and cut them into short pieces of equal length. Tie in bundles and cook in boiling salted water until tender. Drain and cool the stems, chop them into a bowl and cover with an oil and vinegar dressing.

71

Burdock (great burdock)

Botanical name: *Arctium lappa* Family: *Compositae*

Burdock is a handsome native biennial up to 1m (3ft) high with stout, solid stems. The hairy, rhubarb-like leaves start a pale blue-green and become darker green as they grow larger. Flat clusters of purple flowers, 2½–3cm (1–1½in) across, appear in July and develop into the familiar 'burrs' or fruits, which stick to everything they touch.

Burdock contains vitamins A, B and C, iron, calcium and various active substances with healing properties, making it a valuable culinary and medicinal plant. A fairly common wild plant everywhere except in the far north, burdock is found on scrubland, edges of woods, along roadsides and in hedgebanks. Pick stalks before the plant flowers; collect heads for seeds when the fruits are a brownish grey colour.

USES

Only the *young* leaves of burdock are edible. Wash them thoroughly, steam and serve them hot. Or chop them raw in salads.

Young stalks must be washed and peeled before tying in bundles to cook like asparagus. The sweetish-tasting stems may also be candied, as in the recipe below.

The whole plant may be cut up and juiced in a blender, providing a highly nutritious and concentrated liquid for adding to soups and stews.

Even the burrs or hooked seeds have a use; cut ripe burdock heads and hang them upside down in a paper bag to catch the seeds. Allow the seeds to dry and store them for winter sprouters.

Candied burdock

Cut young stalks before the flowers open and wash if necessary. Peel off the rind and cut stems into short lengths. Cover with water, bring to the boil and simmer until tender.

Make a heavy syrup using 275ml (½pt) water to 450g (1lb) sugar. Soak the stems in the syrup for an hour, add a little green colouring and cook until they become transparent.

Drain and when thoroughly dry store in screwtop jars.

Charlock (field mustard)

Botanical name: *Sinapsis arvensis* or *Brassica arvensis* Family: *Cruciferae*

Charlock is the bright-yellow-flowered field weed hated by farmers. Its seeds can remain buried for up to fifty years and still germinate when grassland is ploughed up. Charlock grows to a height of 30–60cm (1–2ft) and is generally bristly with broad toothed, cabbage-like leaves. The four-petalled flowers bloom from April to October and are followed by long angular seed pods containing a row of brown seeds.

Charlock is found in all parts of the country on arable fields and waste places, among grass and by roadsides.

USES
Pick young leaves for spinach. Cook like daisy greens, see page 77.

Charlock

Collect the ripe seeds for winter sprouters. Store them in airtight containers in a cool place.

Chickweed

Botanical name: *Stellaria media* Family: *Caryophyllaceae*

Chickweed is a short, low annual of straggly, prostrate growth. The weak, many-branched stem trails on the ground and has a line of hairs on one side only, alternating sides between each pair of leaves. Shiny and pale green in colour, the succulent, oval-shaped leaves have flat downy stalks, the lower pairs of leaves having longer stalks. The tiny, single white flowers with their five deeply lobed petals are said to open at 9am and on bright days remain facing the sun for twelve hours.

This abundant weed is rich in iron and copper and has a delicate fresh taste like young pea pods. Chickweed is constantly flowering and reseeding and can be found nearly all the year round on bare as well as cultivated ground, often growing on rubbish tips and compost heaps.

USES
Chickweed leaves are so small that it is best to pick bunches of the plant for cooking as a vegetable.

For salads, strip the succulent little leaves off the stems and add whole, or use in sandwiches instead of cress.

Chickweed sandwiches
Wash and chop, or cut up finely, fresh young chickweed leaves. Add 1 tablespoon of leaves to 120g (4oz) softened butter with a few drops of lemon juice. Blend it well together and use in brown-bread sandwiches.

Common reed

Botanical name: *Phragmites communis* Family: *Gramineae*

The common reed is a very tall, waterside perennial grass with stout stems up to 3m (10ft) high and spreading roots. The dense flowerheads, up to 25cm (10in) long, carry numerous purplish spikelets on one side of the many branches from August onwards. These fade to brown and as the fruits form, reveal long silky hairs on the stalks. The long broad leaves die down and the stiff stems remain all winter as bare canes.

Common reed is widespread and grows in large thick beds in shallow, brackish swamps, in freshwater ponds and on edges of marshes.

USES

The rootstock of this large reed has a sweet flavour and should be treated like couchgrass rhizomes. When dry, grind the roots fairly coarsely and use them for making a nourishing porridge.

Corn salad (lamb's lettuce)

Botanical name: *Valerianella locusta* or *olitoria* Family: *Valerianaceae*

The long, narrow leaves of corn salad provide salad greens all the year round. Corn salad is very popular on the Continent where it is sold in the markets, and it can easily be grown in British gardens. It is a short, hairless low-growing annual with many branches and its stalkless, oblong leaves grow directly from the root when they first appear in January or February. From April to June the tiny clusters of greenish-white flowers, with pale lilac corollas, are so small that they look almost colourless. These are followed by a three-chambered seed pod.

Corn salad grows abundantly in the wild, in cultivated fields, in hedges and on railway banks, especially where the soil is dry.

USES

Corn salad is well worth looking for, even under snow, in winter to add nutritious leaves to enrich a salad.

Corn salad with beetroot

Choose young tender leaves, wash lightly. Roughly chop the leaves and mix with a raw grated beetroot.

Toss salad in an oil and vinegar dressing.

Couchgrass (twitchgrass)

Botanical name: *Agropyron repens* Family: *Gramineae*

Couchgrass is a tall, perennial grass. Its spreading root system produces several stems with a beardless, flowering top, rather like rye grass.

The rhizome of couchgrass contains vitamins A and B, as well as organic acids, potassium salts and a carbohydrate substance, which is not a starch. Couchgrass abounds everywhere, a tenacious, spreading weed of fields, roadsides, garden lawns and borders.

USES

Couchgrass may well come in useful in times of shortage for its nutritious, edible rhizome, which can be dried and made into flour to eke out home supplies. Dig up the plant in autumn, remove leaves and rootlets from the swollen rhizomes and dry the rhizomes in a low oven until crisp enough to grind into flour.

Daisy

Botanical name: *Bellis perennis* Family: *Compositae*

Do not despise the common daisy, though it will be difficult to persuade a proud lawn owner of the value of this persistent weed! A hairy perennial, its spoon-shaped leaves grow from a basal rosette. The solitary, white daisy flowers, often with red-tipped petals, grow on leafless stalks.

Although the flavour of the young leaves is somewhat acid, their content of calcium and magnesium makes them a valuable addition to the diet.

USES

Use young daisy leaves raw in spring salads. The leaves are excellent as a cooked spring vegetable, and in soups and sauces and as a flavouring or seasoning.

Some countries use daisy leaves as a pot-herb—a vegetable used to flavour dishes.

Daisy greens
Pick young daisy leaves and wash them quickly in slightly salted water. Put a little water in a pan and add a small pinch of salt. When boiling put in the greens. Cover and cook for about 7–10 minutes.
Serve with a dab of butter and freshly ground black pepper.

Dandelion

Botanical name: *Taraxacum officinalis* Family: *Compositae*

One of our most abundant common weeds, the perennial dandelion has a long flowering season from March to September, or even longer after a mild winter. The leaves start from a basal rosette, their long-toothed lobes pointing backwards. The golden-yellow flowers grow on a single straight stalk which is hollow and, like the root, contains a milky juice. The flowers consist entirely of ray florets, which develop into the familiar fluffy seed heads or 'clocks'. There are a number of similarly related plants with edible leaves, such as cat's ear, nipplewort, hawkbit (p83) goatsbeard (p80) and corn sow-thistle (p105).

Dandelion leaves are rich in active and bitter substances as well as vitamins, proteins, minerals and mineral salts. Dandelions spread freely on the wind and grow in profusion, especially in April and May, in all grassy and waste places, and on lawns.

USES
When there are plenty of dandelions, select a few strong plants and blanch the leaves to provide tender and nutritious greenery for winter salads. To blanch, put a pot over the growing plant, earth up as for cultivated celery; or dig up large roots, pot them up and keep in a warm, dark place until the pale leaves are ready to pick.

Dandelion leaves picked before the plant flowers are the best for salads, and also make an excellent spinach.

Add them to sorrel and nettle leaves for a healthy spring soup. Just tear off the leaves from the stem without digging up the whole plant—new leaves will quickly form. Dandelion roots are also edible. Scrub and chop them into thin slices and stew gently in stock until tender.

For a caffeine-free coffee substitute, dry the roots until quite brittle, then grind them coarsely. Roast the grounds and make coffee in the usual way.

Dandelion flowers make a pleasant herb tea. Use flowerbuds and infuse them in boiling water for 5–10 minutes.

The flowers also make a sweet wine; or mix dandelion petals with roots and leaves to brew dandelion beer.

Dandelion beer

225g (½lb) roots and leaves and 50g (2oz) petals
25g (1oz) ginger, well bruised
4½l (1gall) water
1 lemon

450g (1lb) demerara sugar
12g (½oz) fresh yeast spread on toast
25g (1oz) cream of tartar

Put sugar, cream of tartar and sliced lemon in a large bowl or earthenware crock. Scrub the roots well and wash the leaves. Dry them in a cloth and put in a pan with the petals, the water and ginger, and bring it to the boil. Boil for 10 minutes and pour over ingredients in the bowl. When almost cold add the yeast and leave for 12 hours. Strain off the beer carefully. After three days pour the beer into screwtop bottles.

Can be used after a week.

Evening primrose (lesser evening primrose)

Botanical name: *Oenothera biennis* Family: *Onagraceae*

This handsome biennial plant, of which there are several varieties, has yellow, trumpet-shaped flowers with four petals and reddish sepals. The alternate lanceolate leaves have serrated edges. The evening primrose is not a true wild plant but is sometimes found on dunes, along roadsides and as 'escapes' near gardens. It flowers from June to September.

USES
The value of evening primrose is in its sweet-tasting root, ready for eating at the end of the first season. It has a flavour not unlike parsnips and should be treated like salsify.

Young shoots of the evening primrose can also be eaten raw in salads.

Fat hen

Botanical name: *Chenopodium album*
Chenopodium bonus-henricus—Good King Henry, mercury
Chenopodium polyspermum—many-seeded goosefoot
Chenopodium ficifolium—fig-leaved goosefoot
Chenopodium rubrum—red goosefoot
Family: *Chenopodiaceae*

Fat hen is a native annual growing up to a metre (3ft) high, with deep green diamond- or lance-shaped leaves. In June it produces a spike of tiny, inconspicuous, pale-green flowers which, by late autumn, develop into masses of shiny black seeds.

Good King Henry is an introduced perennial and looks very like fat hen, the same height but with larger, arrow-shaped leaves.

The goosefoots, though rare, are similar to fat hen and Good King Henry and also have edible leaves.

Good King Henry and fat hen are valuable food plants with many uses, exceptionally rich in vitamin B1, iron, calcium and protein—more than cabbage or spinach. Both species grow abundantly on waste places, along roadsides, in arable fields and wherever ground is cultivated, especially near compost heaps.

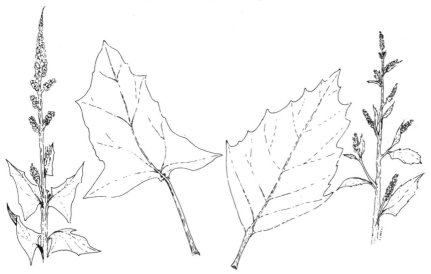

Good King Henry (left) and Fat Hen

The leaves of fat hen and Good King Henry can be eaten raw or cooked. Use them to make a nourishing green soup or as a spinach substitute.

Make fritters with cooked, puréed leaves, soft breadcrumbs, seasoning and an egg to bind the mixture. Shape into flat cakes, dip in seasoned flour, then in thick batter and fry in hot fat.

In the past, the seeds of fat hen were ground to a flour for making bread and cakes, or as a kind of porridge tasting like buckwheat. Caution: never eat the roots of these plants.

Fat hen with cheese
Gather the tips of the side shoots together with the lower leaves from the main stem. Wash and cook them, like spinach, in a small amount of water until tender, about 7–10 minutes. Drain, and press the fat hen between two plates.

Cut into squares and sprinkle grated cheese on top.

Goatsbeard (yellow goatsbeard, Jack-go-to-bed-at-noon)

Botanical name: *Tragopogon pratensis*
Tragopogon porrifolius—salsify, vegetable oyster
Family: *Compositae*

Goatsbeard is an annual or perennial, growing up to 60cm (2ft) high, with a long tap root. The narrow, grass-like leaves sheath the stem, the upper leaves being much shorter than those at the lower end. From June onwards, each stem is topped by a single bright-yellow flower, which opens early and closes at noon. The flower, composed of ray florets like a dandelion, is set in a green sheath consisting of eight slender leaf bracts which spread out as the flower opens, extending beyond the petals. Later, the bracts elongate and swell at the base, finally producing a fluffy 'clock' of seeds which scatter on the wind.

Salsify, a biennial, is very similar to goatsbeard but altogether a larger plant and with purple or pink flowers. It was developed and cultivated from the wild, original, yellow goatsbeard for its long edible root. Its fishy flavour earned it the name of vegetable oyster.

Goatsbeard is extremely common in England and Wales, flourish-

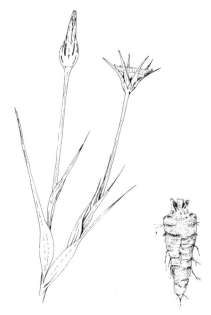

Goatsbeard

ing along roadsides, in meadows, on wasteland and sand dunes.

Salsify is more often found near the sea and estuaries in the south east.

Goatsbeard roots taste like parsnips, for which they are an excellent substitute, prepared and cooked in the same way. Keep them white when peeling by sprinkling with lemon juice. Boil or steam the roots, toss in butter and lemon juice. Or dip them in a thick batter, shallow or deep fry and serve with a herb sauce.

Young goatsbeard leaves and roots are sweet and good to eat raw, or add grated or cubed to salads.

The vegetable oyster has an extraordinary fishy, salty flavour combined with a bittersweet taste. Use in the same ways as goatsbeard. If salsify does not grow wild in your area it may be possible to buy it from an enterprising greengrocer; it is similar to the more easily obtainable scorzonera.

81

The roots of goatsbeard and salsify store well for later use. Lift them in the autumn, twist off stem and leaves, lay the roots in boxes and cover them with a layer of sand. Store away from light and frost.

Creamed goatsbeard roots
Wash, peel and cut the roots into small pieces of equal length. Sprinkle with lemon juice to keep the roots white. Put into a pan with chicken or vegetable stock to cover and cook until tender.

Drain, pour a little melted butter over the top and sprinkle with fresh chopped parsley before serving.

Ground elder (herb gerard, goutweed, bishop's elder)

Botanical name: *Aegopodium podagraria* Family: *Umbelliferae*

Ground elder is a tall perennial umbellifer up to 60cm (2ft) in height. Its deep string-like roots spread relentlessly. From June onwards, it is easily identified by its bractless, white flowers growing in flat

Ground elder

'umbrella' heads on top of hairless stalks; these are followed by ridged, egg-shaped fruits. The large, bright-green, sharply toothed, oval leaves grow in threes at the end of leaf stalks. They are similar in shape and size to the leaves of the common elder shrub, but are not related.

Once cultivated as a pot-herb, ground elder now grows freely in shady and waste places, often in big patches. It is a tenacious garden weed, difficult to eradicate.

USES

The young green leaves of ground elder make an excellent cooked spinach. The rather spicy flavour makes them equally good raw in salads and for seasoning and flavouring soups or stews.

Ground elder in tomato sauce

Gather only the young leaves, then wash and cook them until tender in slightly salted boiling water. Drain and chop them finely. Heat a little oil in a pan and add a small finely chopped onion, cover and cook until tender but still white. Stir in a sprinkle of flour and a little stock to make a smooth sauce. Add a teaspoon of tomato purée and lastly the ground elder. Stir whilst it heats through.

Serve very hot.

Hawkbit (rough hawkbit, greater hawkbit)

Botanical name: *Leontodon hispidus* Family: *Compositae*

The hawkbits are related to and look like dandelions. A native perennial, rough hawkbit grows to about 50cm (18in) in height. It has single yellow flowers, a little smaller than dandelions and occasionally red or orange beneath. The buds first appear on a drooping stem, which eventually grows erect when the flower opens in May. It will continue flowering through to September or October.

Rough hawkbit grows mostly in England and is common on chalk meadows, grassy slopes and roadside verges.

USES

Use the leaves in the same way as dandelion in salads, or as a cooked vegetable.

Hawkbit salad
Gather young hawkbit leaves and soak overnight. Drain and dry them in a clean cloth. Chop the leaves and place in a salad bowl with some chopped chives. Add an oil and vinegar dressing, and sprinkle a few dandelion petals on top.

Herb bennet

Botanical name: *Geum urbanum* Family: *Rosaceae*

A shade-loving plant, herb bennet is used for its roots, which smell and taste like cloves. It is a downy perennial growing up to 60cm (2ft) high, and has tiny yellow, five-petalled flowers appearing in May. These are followed in September by fruit heads consisting of a mass of reddish, single-seeded fruits ending in hooks, which catch on to passing birds and animals as a means of distribution. The beautiful trefoil leaves are bright green, toothed and pinnate, the bottom leaflets rounded, the top ones long and narrow.

Herb bennet

84

Herb bennet grows everywhere except in the extreme north. It is common in damp woods, hedge banks and other shady places.

USES
Dig up the small roots of herb bennet in spring when they are most sweet and aromatic. Use them to liven up casseroles and soups, or as a clove flavouring. Approximately one handful of roots 5cm (2in) long is equivalent to one clove. The roots may be dried until brittle and then powdered as a substitute for ground cloves in a recipe.

Herb-bennet stuffed apples
Allow 2 or 3 pieces 5cm (2in) long of root to each apple. Remove the apple cores. Wash the roots and chop them up finely. Mix together a tablespoon each of softened butter, sugar, wholemeal flour or ground almonds and add the herb bennet roots. Fill the apples with the mixture and bake in a moderate oven 180°C (350°F, Gas 4) until soft, about 40–45 minutes.

Hops

Botanical name: *Humulus lupulus* Family: *Cannabinaceae*

Normally cultivated for the brewing of beer, hops are a member of the hemp family and are often found growing wild. They are perennial plants climbing clockwise up and over hedges, thickets and trees near to areas where they are cultivated. The prickly, heart-shaped leaves, rather like vine leaves, grow in pairs on square stems. The small flowers, male and female, grow on separate plants; the former are greenish-white and grow in loose bunches. The female flowers, used for beer making, form inside cone-shaped catkins which increase rapidly in size from about July onwards, and turn brown by autumn. They contain a bitter substance, lupulin, which gives the flowers their fragrance, especially when bruised.

Hops may be found in thickets and tall hedges, but do not confuse them with the poisonous white or black bryony. In cultivation, many of the hop shoots have to be removed to allow the plant to develop, so if you live near hop fields these cuttings make a delicious vegetable.

85

Hops—female flowers (top), male flowers and shoots

USES
The female flowers can be gathered in autumn, dried and used for adding to home-brewed beer.

A pleasing wine may also be made from hop flowers. Dry hops in the usual way and use them for making a sedative tea for inducing sleep. Pour 575ml (1pt) boiling water on to a handful of dried hops and allow to steep a few minutes before straining.

Hop shoots, picked not later than May, make an excellent cooked vegetable. Add them to sauces and spring soups.

Hop shoots
Gather the hop shoots in early spring, wash them well and tie in bundles. Cook in boiling water until tender. Drain, serve with a butter sauce and eat the shoots like asparagus.

86

Lady's smock (cuckoo flower)

Botanical name: *Cardamine pratensis* Family: *Cruciferae*

A member of the bittercress family, lady's smock is a hairless, medium-sized perennial. From a basal rosette the pinnate root leaves grow in opposite pairs. The four-petalled flowers, white or pale lilac, grow in corymbs, which elongate into fruit pods containing a single row of seeds.

Lady's smock is rich in vitamin C and is pungently bitter. A common wild flower throughout Britain, it grows in meadows, along stream-sides and other damp places. Do not overpick this plant, for orange-tip butterfly larvae feed on its flowers: pick some leaves off the stem and leave the plant to grow on.

USES

Lady's smock makes an excellent substitute for watercress, which it resembles. Chop it raw into salads and sandwiches.

It may also be boiled and eaten as a vegetable, or used in spring soups.

Spring soup

1 large onion or 2–3 spring onions	1 small bunch sorrel
2 potatoes	1 small bunch spinach
1 tablespoon mixed wild herbs	milk and water
1 small bunch lady's smock	oil

Peel and chop the onion and potatoes and sauté lightly in oil. Stir in mixed herbs and sauté a little longer. Wash and chop the lady's smock, spinach and sorrel and add them to the pan. Cover well with equal quantities of milk and water. Simmer until vegetables are quite soft. Cool and put soup through the electric blender.

Re-heat, season to taste and serve with fried bread or croutons.

Mallow

Botanical name: *Malva sylvestris* Family: *Malvaceae*

A handsome, common perennial or biennial, mallow has a stout, hairy, rather sprawling stem. From June to September the large, elegant, pale-mauve flowers, purple-veined, bloom only one or two at a time. Their five petals, with a deep notch in the outer edge, are arranged in an open formation so that the lobes of the green calyx can be seen between each petal. The stamens join to form a small purple pillar which gradually opens out into a spray of anthers and stigmas.

The large, crinkly leaves, rather like hands with five blunt points, are coarse and downy, those near the root having a dark purple blotch near the centre.

Mallow leaves contain vitamins A, C, B1 and B2 and a certain amount of mucilage. Mallow is found on rough ground, along roadsides and on banks, mostly in the south, often near the sea.

USES

When boiled, mallow leaves make a natural thickener for soups and sauces. If picked young enough, the cooked leaves also provide a nourishing vegetable, but when old are not so pleasant. They need washing well before chopping up finely.

For a nourishing thick soup first cook the chopped leaves for ten minutes in plenty of stock. Proceed as for nettle soup.

The ripe seeds of mallow are also edible and have a good nutty flavour. Country children like to eat them raw.

Marsh woundwort

Botanical name: *Stachys palustris* Family: *Labiatae*

Marsh woundwort is a useful wild plant for its edible roots and stems. It is a creeping, hairy perennial with unbranched stems of 60–90cm (2–3ft) growing straight from the rhizome. The toothed, lance-shaped leaves grow in pairs at intervals up the stout, hollow stem. At the top, pale lilac flowers grow in whorled spikes, about six to a whorl, starting in July. The underground rhizome, with its masses of white rootlets, extends in all directions, throwing up numerous shoots.

Marsh woundwort, an arable weed, is common locally in ditches, marshes and fens, beside ponds and streams.

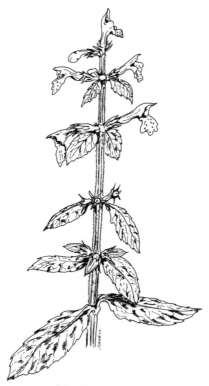

Marsh woundwort

Once widely used as a healing plant, marsh woundwort can provide an excellent, nutritious root vegetable, white and crisp with a
pleasant flavour. The root may also be dried until brittle and ground
to flour or meal.

The stems can be cooked like asparagus. Treat like hop shoots,
page 86.

Marsh woundwort root salad
Dig up some roots and scrub them well. Put them into slightly
salted boiling water and cook until tender. Leave to cool, then chop
up the roots roughly. Serve as a salad in an oil and lemon dressing
and sprinkle with flavouring herbs.

Nettle

Botanical name: *Urtica dioica*—Stinging nettle
Urtica urens—Small nettle
Family: *Urticaceae*

Lamium album—White dead-nettle
Family: *Labiatae*

Stinging nettles grow up to 1½m (5ft) in height and have a tough, spreading root system. The stem, as well as the toothed, heart-shaped leaves, is covered in stinging hairs. The catkins of small flowers are green with yellow stamens and appear in June, with male and female flowers on separate plants.

The small nettle, an annual, is very similar to the stinging nettle but less hairy and with smaller, rounder leaves. Male and female catkins grow on the same plant.

The white dead-nettle, a perennial weed, has leaves the same shape and size as stinging nettle leaves but without the stinging hairs. The whole plant is faintly aromatic. From March onwards, largish white flowers with an upper and divided lower lip, grow in the lower leaf axils.

Stinging nettles are a rich source of nutrients and minerals, especially vitamins A and C, as well as some protein. The sting in the hairs is produced by the presence of formic acid, destroyed immediately by boiling or washing.

A very common weed everywhere, stinging nettles grow abundantly on rubbish tips, compost heaps and disturbed ground. The small annual nettle is widespread on lighter soils, and the white dead-nettle is common in hedgebanks and along roadsides.

USES

Use gloves to pick young nettle shoots as soon as they appear in early spring. Their value deteriorates once the plant flowers as they get tough and bitter, even laxative. Quickly wash and chop the leaves into spring salads.

Cook nettle leaves like spinach, or mix with cultivated spinach to make it go further. The salty flavour of nettles makes them a useful ingredient in a salt-free diet. Used as a herb, fresh or dried, nettles flavour stews, sauces, stuffings, dumplings and savoury puddings. They also make a delicious green soup when puréed and flavoured as suggested in the recipe.

A substitute for rennet, to set junket and puddings, can be made from nettle juice. A spoonful of nettle decoction will coagulate a large bowl of milk. Pour cold water over nettles in a saucepan and bring to boil. Boil for 20–30 minutes. Cool and strain.

Nettle wine and beer are well worth making. (See recipe in Chapter 2.)

Use small nettles in the same ways as the larger variety. White dead-nettle shoots, picked early in the spring, make a good spinach vegetable. Nettle leaves dry well; follow the method on page 30. Store in airtight jars away from light.

In the garden nettles have their value for enriching soil with nitrogen, stimulating the growth of other plants growing nearby and bringing out the essential oils in aromatic herbs. They are also an ideal weed for raising heat in the compost heap and make perfect humus as a mulch and fertiliser in the vegetable plot.

Nettle soup
Pick young nettle leaves when the plants are 15–20cm high (6–8in). Wear gloves to protect the hands. Wash the nettles in running water, drain and chop finely. Put a little water in a pan, add the nettles and simmer until tender, about 10 minutes. Cool and put through an electric blender. Melt a little butter in the pan, sauté 1 finely chopped onion and 1 minced clove of garlic until soft. Add enough flour to make a roux, stir and cook a few minutes. Gradually add 575ml (1pt) of hot milk and water, stirring until smooth.

Add the nettle purée, season to taste and bring to the boil. Simmer for 10 minutes.

Orpine (large stonecrop, livelong)

Botanical name: *Sedum telephium* Family: *Crassulaceae*

The fleshy leaves of the large stonecrop, a succulent plant, will remain alive and green long after they have been picked. Orpine grows to about 30cm (1ft) high. It has numerous broad, oblong leaves, coarsely toothed and growing alternately and densely up the solid reddish-brown stems. Bluish-green in colour, the upper leaves are stalkless and the lower ones taper to short foot stalks. From July to September, the crimson or rose-coloured flowers with their spreading petals form broad heads at the top of each stem.

Orpine has astringent properties and contains mucilage and various mineral elements. It is fairly widespread in woods and hedges. Cultivated garden varieties are similar but larger.

USES

The leaves and roots of orpine make good vegetables, especially in soups and stews for adding nutrients and flavour. Young leaves may also be used raw in small amounts in a mixed green salad.

Pignut (earthnut)

Botanical name: Conopodium majus Family: Umbelliferae

The bulbous root of this native perennial plant, once much sought after by country children, may be found 5–7cm (2–3in) below ground. Above ground pignut appears as a wispy little umbellifer with a hollow stem about 30cm (1ft) tall. It grows directly from the brown tuber. The two or three delicate pinnate leaves are narrow and often sparse. The bractless white flowers bloom from May to July.

Pignuts may be found in all parts of Britain, chiefly in woods, hedgebanks and fields, but not on chalky soil.

Pignut (earthnut)—with root

92

To dig up pignuts, do not try pulling by the stem which will break off immediately. Once identified, dig down beside the plant with an old kitchen knife or fork and work the tuber out carefully. Clean off dirt, scrape, then wash the tubers and eat them raw. They are delicious and taste like chestnuts. They may be boiled in seasoned stock or broth and served as a vegetable. Add to soups or stews.

Plantain

Botanical name: *Plantago major*—waybread, greater plantain
Plantago lanceolata—ribwort plantain, 'soldiers'
Family: *Plantaginaceae*

Greater plantain is a perennial weed, 15cm (6in) in height, its large, ribbed, oval leaves growing from a rosette in the ground. The pinky-purplish flowers grow densely on long, straight spikes, the flowering part longer than its stalk. It flowers in June and July.

Ribwort plantain flowers from April to August, its flower spikes are shorter and more compact, brown in colour with light yellow anthers. It has a deeply furrowed stalk and the leaves are lance-shaped and ribbed with three to six veins.

Both plantains grow tiresomely on lawns and abundantly in most open spaces and along roadsides.

USES

Plantain leaves make a good spinach, but must be well cooked. Gather only the young leaves for chopping raw into a salad, otherwise you may find them rather tough and bitter.

Purslane

Botanical name: *Portulaca oleracea*
Claytonia (Montia) perfoliata—winter purslane, spring beauty
Family: *Portulacaceae*

A half-hardy annual, purslane is a low, spreading plant with small, oval leaves, which are thick and fleshy. In July the yellow flowers appear on erect stems.

Purslane; on left, winter purslane or spring beauty

Winter purslane is a small annual with little white flowers and perfoliate leaves—leaves with the stalks going through them.

Purslane contains vitamins, minerals and trace elements and is one of the most valuable wild plants. Common purslane is found in dry sandy places throughout Britain. Winter purslane is widespread on sandy soils and cultivated places.

USES

The tasty leaves and stems of purslane make an excellent cooked vegetable or a raw salad ingredient. Strip the leaves from the stalks and use them to make nutritious brown-bread sandwiches.

The leaves and stems of winter purslane are also good for salads, or as a first-class spinach. Cook like daisy greens, page 77. Purslane leaves dry well for storing. See page 29 for directions.

Purslane salad herb

In spring when the plant is tender and succulent, use the leaves and young shoots chopped in salads.

Purslane pot herb
In summer and early autumn use the older shoots to flavour a lamb casserole.

Purslane pickle
In late autumn cut the thick stems, peel off the outer skin and chop them small. Boil till tender. Drain and cover with boiling wine vinegar and cider in equal quantities. Cover and put in a slow oven 150°C (300°F, Gas 2) for one hour.

Samphire (sea fennel, rock samphire)

Botanical name: *Crithmum maritimum* Family: *Umbelliferae*

There are several kinds of samphire growing in salt marshes round our coasts, but rock samphire or sea fennel is a well-known

Rock samphire

delicacy, as succulent as asparagus. It is also used as a pickle. It should not be confused with marsh samphire (*Salicornia herbacea*), a different species but one that is also eaten as a vegetable or pickle (see page 99).

Rock samphire is a hardy perennial growing to 30cm (1ft) or more, and has many branched, jointed stems, greyish and solid, sometimes woody at the base. The fleshy leaves are triangular and pointed, each with a thick sheath encircling the stem at the base. Tiny yellowish-green flowers grow in umbels and develop into large, purply-green, ridged fruits.

Rock samphire is not very common, but is found on cliffs and shingles, in Cornwall, South Wales and the South of Ireland.

USES

The leaves of samphire can be eaten raw as a salty appetiser, or boiled and served hot or cold with bread and butter. Cook samphire like asparagus, first removing any sodden leaves and hard pieces of stalk. Samphire requires about fifteen minutes cooking. Follow the recipe for hop shoots. Samphire seeds, as well as the leaves, make a good pickle.

Scurvy grass

Botanical name: *Cochlearia officinalis*
Cochlearia alpina
Cochlearia anglica
Cochlearia danica
Family: *Cruciferae*

Four varieties of scurvy grass grow in Britain, each growing in a different part of the country.

Common scurvy grass is a small native plant up to 30cm (1ft) high. Its heart-shaped root leaves are fleshy, dark green and smooth-edged. The upper leaves cling to the stem and are more pointed than those lower down. The insignificant little flowers are mostly white, sometimes pale lilac, and are followed by small, semi-transparent, round seed pods.

Cochlearia alpina has less fleshy leaves and horizontal stems up to 45cm (18in) long. The variety *anglica* has longer, narrower leaves and larger flowers than the common scurvy grass, and *Cochlearia*

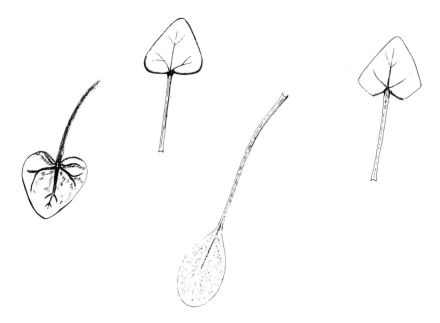

Scurvy grass: left to right, *Cochlearia danica*, *C. officinalis* (the common scurvy grass), *C. anglica*, *C. alpina*

danica, the only annual variety, bears lilac flowers early in the year. Its leaves are stalked, the lower ones more heart-shaped.

Scurvy grass leaves contain one of the richest sources of vitamin C, or ascorbic acid.

Common scurvy grass grows mostly on sea cliffs and brackish marshes round all our coasts except in the south. *C. alpina* grows wild in all highland areas; *C. anglica* is rare but sometimes found on muddy shores and estuaries in the south; *C. danica* can be found on sand, banks, rocks and among pebbles along the west coast during the winter months.

USES

Whichever variety you find, make use of this vitamin-rich plant. Although the leaves are bitter tasting, just a few fresh or dried, chopped finely, will enrich a salad. A drink can also be made of the dried leaves. For drying, see page 29.

Sea plants

Botanical name: *Beta maritima*—sea beet, sea spinach
Halimione portulacoides—sea purslane, grey mat
Salicornia herbacea—marsh samphire, glasswort
Family: *Chenopodiaceae*
Crambe maritima—sea kale
Family: *Cruciferae*

Sea beet or sea spinach, belonging to the goosefoot family, is a wild species of cultivated beets and can be annual, biennial or perennial. Tall and hairless, it grows up to 1m (3ft) high and has dark green, untoothed shiny leaves, large and fleshy near the base of the plant, the upper leaves thinner and spear shaped. They are sometimes red-veined, like the cultivated beet greens. In May it produces long spikes of small, petalless greeny flowers with yellow anthers and joined sepals.

Sea purslane is a woody perennial, height up to 80cm (2½ft), with silvery grey, untoothed, elliptical leaves covered in bladder-like hairs resembling grey 'meal'. It grows in a straggly fashion and is many-branched. In July it produces small yellowish-green flowers on short slender sprays, male and female flowers on the same plant.

Marsh samphire's synonym, glasswort, derives from an earlier use, for its ashes contain carbonate of soda, used in glass-making. Marsh samphire is a small, erect annual and looks more like a cactus with its fat, leafless, jointed stems, each branch ending in a spike. The flowers, the same green colour as the stems, are barely visible and grow in the intervals between branch and stem.

Sea kale, a member of the cabbage family, has a curly, cabbage-like leaf and grows from a brown woody stump of a rootstock, visible on shingle and rocks in winter. From May to August it produces big heads of fragrant white flowers on thick stems.

The most easily found and valuable sea plant, from the nutritional point of view, is the sea beet, rich in vitamins A and C. Sea beet grows commonly at the edges of seashores and salt marshes round all coasts except Scotland and northern England.

Sea purslane is also found in salt marshes and at the edges of pools and creeks. It is more common in east and south-east England and Wales. Glasswort or marsh samphire is only found in coastal areas of south and east England. Sea kale is rarer and mostly found along the eastern shores of the English coast.

In order to preserve the valuable nutrients in sea beet, cook the larger leaves as little as possible. Better still, pick young leaves near the top of the plant before it flowers and chop them raw in a salad.

Sea purslane leaves are also quite palatable in salads, but be sure to wash them well and do not pick any from polluted areas.

Marsh samphire, although not in the same class as rock samphire, is eaten as a boiled vegetable, or may be pickled. Always wash marsh samphire well in plenty of fresh water before using.

Pick young shoots of sea kale when they first appear and are large enough to make a dish. Cook in lightly salted boiling water until tender and serve with butter sauce, a sprinkle of lemon juice and freshly ground black pepper.

Sea spinach tart

Make a purée of sea spinach leaves (see nettle, page 90). Allow to cool completely. Line a flan case with shortcrust pastry. Mix the purée with a beaten egg and season to taste. Fill the pastry case with the spinach and bake in a moderate oven 190°C (375°F, Gas 5) for about 30 minutes.

Serve hot as a supper dish, or to eat cold cover the tart thickly with chopped hard-boiled egg.

Sea purslane leaves in a green salad

Choose the young succulent leaves and wash them well. Add in small quantities to mixed green salads.

Sea kale stems

Strip the leaves from the stems and wash well, removing any decayed pieces. Tie in small bundles and put into boiling salted water. Cook until tender. Drain, remove string and serve hot with a white sauce, or if liked a Hollandaise sauce.

Marsh samphire pickle

Wash the samphire well in plenty of water. Cut into short lengths, put it into an earthenware jar or bowl and cover with boiling vinegar and light wine or water in equal quantities. Cover and leave in a slow oven for one hour 140°C (275°F, Gas 1).

Shepherd's purse

Botanical name: *Capsella bursa pastoris* Family: *Cruciferae*

Shepherd's purse is a widespread annual weed, which flowers all
the year round, varying considerably in height and form according
to the quality of the soil. Its base leaves grow close to the ground and
may be deeply toothed or nearly undivided. A few smaller oblong
leaves, arrow-shaped at the base, clasp the slender stem, which is
35–60cm (14–24in) tall. The numerous little white flowers are followed by the characteristic heart-shaped, triangular seed pods said
to resemble a shepherd's purse of bygone days. As they ripen, the
pods separate into two cells, each containing many long yellow
seeds.

Shepherd's purse contains vitamin C and the important mineral
calcium. It also has stimulating properties which are valuable in
medicines. A self-perpetuating plant, shepherd's purse flourishes
in any kind of soil and is found in every type of habitat, from cultivated gardens to the wildest places.

Shepherd's purse

USES

The flavour of shepherd's purse leaves is aromatic and pungent, not unlike cress. The lower leaves make a rather spicy, good cabbage vegetable. They can also be chopped raw and added to other salad greens. Use the raw herb in place of cress in sandwiches or as a garnish.

When dried, shepherd's purse leaves make a peppery flavouring or substitute useful for soups and sauces. Dry and store the leaves in the usual way.

Shepherd's purse slaw
Wash and drain the lower leaves, shred finely and add to a bowl of shredded green, white or red cabbage. Add a sprinkle of caraway seeds and toss in an oil and vinegar dressing, or mix the salad with a herb-flavoured mayonnaise.

Silverweed

Botanical name: *Potentilla anserina* Family: *Rosaceae*

There are many *Potentillas* or cinquefoils growing wild but the commonest is silverweed, with its highly nutritious starchy root. It is a little prostrate perennial plant 15cm (6in) high with small, yellow, five-petalled flowers looking like buttercups. The feathery, deeply pinnate leaves grow in pairs, alternately large and small. The silky, soft green tops and silvery undersides are created by a covering of white, downy hairs. The extensive root system is the part used.

Silverweed is known to contain the minerals iron, calcium and magnesium and doubtless has other constituents. It was once a well-known medicinal plant for healing many complaints. Silverweed abounds in any soil, preferring damp grass and waste places. It also grows in hedgebanks, fields and on dunes. The flowers start in May but the roots should be dug up in the autumn.

USES
Silverweed roots taste rather like parsnips and were cultivated as a vegetable before the potato was introduced. The roots may be boiled, baked or braised and served hot as a vegetable. They may be added to meat stews and to flavour soups and stocks.

A flour for bread-making may be made from the dried, finely ground roots. This meal also makes quite a nice hot gruel.

Silverweed porridge
Scrub the roots well and put in a pan with cold water. Bring to the boil and simmer until tender. Drain, chop them small and leave to dry in a warm place. When completely dry, grind them to a coarse meal and keep in a screwtop jar.

To make the porridge:

575ml (1pt) warm water   50g (2oz) meal
Salt

Gradually add the meal to the hot salted water in a pan over gentle heat, stirring all the time to keep it smooth. Cover and allow to cook for 20–30 minutes.

Sorrels

Botanical name: *Rumex acetosa*—common or garden sorrel, wild sorrel
Rumex scutatus—French sorrel
Rumex crispus and *R. obtusifolius*—curled and broad leaved dock
Rumex acetosella—sheep's sorrel
Family: *Polygonaceae*

Oxalis acetosella—wood-sorrel
Family: *Oxalidaceae*

Common or wild sorrel is a tall, erect, hairless perennial. The two bottom lobes of the arrow-shaped leaves point backwards. The smaller and narrower upper leaves cling to the reddish-coloured ridged stem. Whorls of the small green flowers growing on branched spikes appear in May, and gradually turn red by June or July. Male and female flowers grow on separate plants.

Sheep's sorrel, a native annual, is very similar in appearance to common sorrel but has much narrower leaves with the lobes pointing forward. It has a longer flowering period up to August, but bears flowers the same colour.

French sorrel is a variety cultivated for its less acid leaves and is used in France for making the famous sorrel soup. It is distinguished from other sorrels by its overall bluish-green bloom and crisp, heart-shaped leaves. From June to July bi-sexual flowers grow on the same plant.

The two docks belonging to the sorrel family are both native perennials and common everywhere. Broad-leaved dock grows up to 90cm (3ft) tall and has broad, oblong leaves with hairy undersides. The flower head is many branched, the flowers more numerous and, like the sorrels, start green and turn red.

Curled dock is similar in size and appearance but its leaves have curled, wavy edges.

Wood-sorrel, although a different species, is included because its leaves are used in the same way as sorrel leaves for their sharp vinegary taste. Wood-sorrel is a dainty little perennial plant with a spreading root system, from which rise the leaf and flower stems, no taller than 15cm (6in). The delicate, lime-green leaves consist of three heart-shaped leaflets, which open in the shade and fold up in direct sunlight or stormy weather. The solitary white flowers with mauve veins have five petals and yellow stamens.

All sorrel leaves are rich in vitamin C and oxalic and other acids. In addition they contain various minerals, especially iron.

Common sorrel is widespread in Britain in woods and meadows and along roadsides. Sheep's sorrel grows everywhere except on chalky soil, preferring heath and grassland. French sorrel may be found as a naturalised wild plant in the north of the country, and is often cultivated in gardens. Docks grow everywhere and are troublesome weeds on farmland and in gardens. They abound on roadsides, waste ground and in hedgebanks. Wood-sorrel is found in woods, hedges and shady places throughout Britain.

USES

Sorrel leaves have a distinctly sharp, even sour, taste and can take the place of lemon or vinegar in salad dressings and sauces. Add chopped raw leaves to sharpen a green salad. Cook and purée the leaves as a vegetable, or use them in a nutritious spring soup (see page 87). This is superb when made with French sorrel if you can find it. Sorrel is also good mixed with nettles and other vegetables as a soup or spinach.

Dock leaves have the same tart flavour and if picked when young make a good cooked vegetable.

Sorrel and dock leaves may be dried and stored in the same way as other leaves and herbs.

Sorrel sauce
Make a purée of sorrel leaves (see nettle page 90). Soften the flavour by mixing sorrel with cream or melted butter. Add salt, pepper and a pinch of sugar to taste. Thin with strong meat stock and serve with chicken or veal.

Tansy

Botanical name: *Tanacetum vulgare* Family: *Compositae*

Tansy is an attractive plant with beautiful fern-like leaves. It is a stiff, stout, almost hairless perennial growing to 1m (3ft) in height, strongly aromatic, redolent of lemon and camphor. From July to September tansy is easy to recognise by its flat heads of golden, button-shaped flowers. The deeply pinnate, toothed leaves are a rich dark green and available most of the year.

Tansy contains some protein, volatile oil, tannins, resin, sugar and a green colouring matter used in dye-making.

Commonly found in most parts of Britain, tansy grows in grassy places, along roadsides, hedgerows and on waste land.

USES
In spite of its lemony aroma, tansy has a particularly bitter flavour, not to everyone's liking. But it was once a widely grown popular herb said to be good for the stomach, traditionally served with cakes and eggs at Easter and in the well known tansy pudding. Tansy leaves were also used to rub over stored meat to keep flies away.

Use a small quantity of finely chopped tansy leaves as a seasoning in meat dishes and stews.

Tansy pudding

275ml (½pt) milk	50g (2oz) sugar
12g (½oz) butter	75g (3oz) breadcrumbs
2 eggs	1 dessertspoon tansy leaves

Boil milk with the butter and pour over the breadcrumbs. Leave for

½ hour. Beat the eggs and mix into breadcrumbs with the sugar and finely chopped young tansy leaves. Pour into a greased pie dish and bake in a medium oven, 180°C (350°F, Gas 4), until the mixture is set. Serve cold with cream.

Thistles

Botanical name: *Cirsium vulgare*—spear thistle
Cirsium arvense—creeping thistle
Cirsium palustre—marsh thistle
Cirsium eriophorum—woolly thistle
Onopordum acanthium—scotch thistle
Silybum marianum—milk or holy thistle
Sonchus arvensis—corn sow thistle
Sonchus oleraceus—common sow or smooth thistle
Family: *Compositae*

The many thistles with edible stems and roots all belong to the *compositae* group of plants but have different latin names. Only brief descriptions are given, so check identification with illustrated books when gathering. The most common of the true thistles are the *cirsiums*, also named *carduus*.

Spear thistles, growing to 1½m (5ft), have long stem leaves which point downwards, with bristly upper sides and tipped with long sharp points. From July to October purple flower-heads sprout from a fat, oval bract covered with spiny points.

Creeping thistle spreads from roots which throw up straight, wingless stems up to 60cm (2ft) or more. The leaves are extremely spiky. From July to September pinkish-purple male and female flowers grow on separate plants. The female flowers have long, hairy bracts.

Marsh thistle has a taller stem winged by leaves with long spines and hairy uppersides. In June, numerous reddish-purple flowers in cottony grey bracts grow at the top of the branching stems and in the leaf axils, with the male and female on one plant.

The woolly thistle is a strong biennial variety up to 1½m (5ft) tall with a many-branched wingless stem which has no prickles. The deeply segmented, spiny-tipped leaves are hairy beneath and unstalked. In August, single purple flower-heads bloom upright on top of a round, woolly-haired bract.

105

Milk thistle

The scotch thistle, covered in white woolly hairs, is a handsome biennial up to 1½m (5ft). It has long, prickly stem leaves growing parallel and attached to the stout stem, but the root leaves are lobed and spiny-toothed. In September the purple flower-head on top of a prickly globe develops tufty hair to carry the seeds far and wide.

The holy or milk thistle is more rare, an annual once much cultivated by the Romans for food and medicine. It grows to 1.2m (4ft) in height; the leaves are a shiny dark green with white veins and spiny edges. The large, solitary purple flowers bloom from June to September but are inclined to droop.

The two sow thistles carry golden-yellow flower heads, similar to dandelions.

Corn sow thistle, a perennial, is a very common spreading weed with a hollow stem containing a milky juice. Its oblong leaves have

106

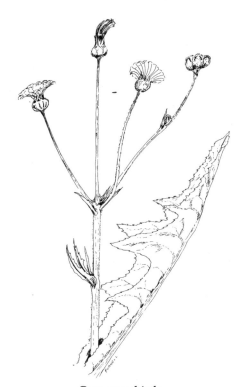

Corn sow thistle

soft spiny lobes. It flowers from July to September.

The smooth sow thistle, a smaller annual, has no prickles on stem or leaf. The outer florets of the small yellow flowers are sometimes tinged purple, and bloom from May or June to October. The seeds form a 'dandelion clock' and spread easily, making this a common weed everywhere.

Most thistles contain important minerals—calcium, copper, iron and potassium—and the two sow thistles also contain the important vitamin C.

From June and July onwards, spear, creeping and marsh thistles can be found throughout Britain in grassy and waste places. The creeping thistle especially is a pestilential weed in arable fields; marsh thistles also grow in wet places. The woolly thistle is more uncommon, mostly found in southern England and Wales on chalky scrub and grassland and in old pits. Milk thistles grow in limestone areas, chiefly near the sea, and naturalised more locally in the Thames estuary. The scotch thistle, surprisingly, is never found in Scotland, but grows mostly in East Anglia and other southern counties along roadsides. Corn sow thistle is widespread on cultivated ground, beside streams and on edges of salt marshes. The smooth sow thistle is more abundant, a tiresome weed on dunes and walls, and any waste or disturbed ground.

USES

The prickly thistles are worth the trouble of gathering and deprickling. Stout stems should be peeled and soaked for a short while to remove traces of bitterness. Then stew them like rhubarb, or tie in bundles, steam and eat like asparagus.

Even the round, spiny bracts surrounding the flower heads, especially milk thistle bracts, may be boiled and eaten like globe artichokes.

The smooth sow thistles are easier to handle and make excellent vegetables. Prickles on the edges of corn sow thistle leaves should be trimmed off and they can then be chopped raw into salads. Their roots are also edible but must be dug up when young, or they will be tough.

Willowherb (rosebay willowherb, fireweed)

Botanical name: *Epilobium angustifolium* Family: *Onagraceae*

Willowherb is a prolific weed but has its uses as a food plant. It grows to a height of 1½m (5ft), is practically hairless and has alternate, narrow, toothed leaves. The rosy or pinky-purple flowers, massed on tall spikes, have unequal petals and long, drooping stamens. They appear in June and by September have ripened into white fluffy seeds, often seen floating or blowing about in the wind.

Common throughout Britain, willowherb can be found in open woods, on heaths, scree, railway banks, waste ground and mountains. When its red flowers appear, this tall perennial is unmistakeable, growing in patches, especially where the ground has been devastated by fire. It was a bright feature of city bombed sites after the last war.

108

USES

The leaves of willowherb are astringent and when infused make a reasonable healthy tea. They are also good as a green vegetable if gathered in the spring.

The shoots, peeled and boiled, may be eaten as an asparagus substitute. Or use leaves and shoots together as a flavouring pot-herb.

The roots, dug up in spring, may also be boiled and eaten as a vegetable or added to meat casseroles. Try willowherb spinach made as the ground-elder recipe on page 83.

5

WILD HERBS FOR FLAVOURING

There are many flavouring herbs growing in the wild as fresh substitutes for the garden varieties and those bought dried.

Balm or lemon balm

Botanical name: *Melissa officinalis* Family: *Labiatae*

A medium-height perennial with pale green, crinkly, heart-shaped leaves. Tiny white flowers, beloved by bees, bloom all summer. The leaves have a lovely lemon scent when pinched and should be picked before the flowers appear. A garden 'escape' in country lanes and waysides near habitation, mostly in the south.

Use for lemon flavour in savoury and sweet dishes, jams and jellies. Fresh or dried leaves make a relaxing bedtime drink. Make like tea: allow 1 teaspoon fresh or dried balm per cup, steep for 5–10 minutes, strain.

Basil

Botanical name: *Clinopodium vulgare* Family: *Labiatae*

A common, hairy perennial with tall square stems, toothed crinkly leaves on short stalks. From July to September rosy-red flowers grow in whorls at end of stem. Found in hedgerows and edges of woods, mainly in southern England.

Leaves provide good substitute for cultivated basil, it has a strong

110

flavour, and goes well with tomatoes, eggs, roast meats, stuffings and a salad dressing.

Borage

Botanical name: *Borago officinalis* Family: *Boraginaceae*

Once cultivated, now a common wild annual, height to 30cm (1ft), it has large, furry, heart-shaped leaves and hairy stems and the brilliant blue starlike flowers are much visited by bees. Borage may be found near houses on waste ground. The leaves, with a subtle cucumber flavour, and flower sprigs make an attractive and tasty addition to salads. Use flowers to float in summer wine cups.

Chervil (Queen Anne's lace, cow parsley)

Botanical name: *Anthriscus sylvestris* Family: *Umbelliferae*.

Height 30–120cm (1–4ft), stems hollow and furrowed, hairy near base only. Bright green, much-divided leaves like ferns, and umbels of tiny white flowers. The first umbellifer to green up in spring. Grows abundantly in ditches, hedgebanks and along country lanes throughout Britain. Do not confuse with the related poisonous fool's parsley and hemlock.

Pick young chervil leaves as soon as they appear, use in place of parsley. Add to bouquets garnis, or on its own to flavour salads, soups, sauces, casseroles and omelettes.

Fennel

Botanical name: *Foeniculum vulgare* Family: *Umbelliferae*

A tall, stout perennial up to 120cm (4ft), with yellow flower heads from July to October. Leaves much divided, look more like green threads. It has a faint anise aroma. Abundant on cliff tops round coasts, especially in the southwest.

The best fish herb and also goes well with all egg dishes. Ripe fennel seeds are good in apple pies—also said to sweeten the breath when chewed.

111

Garlic mustard (Jack-by-the-hedge, hedge garlic)

Botanical name: *Alliaria petiolata* Family:*Cruciferae*

Height up to 120 cm (4ft), a native biennial with bright green, slightly toothed, heart-shaped leaves. The pure white flowers appear from April to June, the shoots may appear as early as February after a mild winter. Plentiful in hedgebanks and edges of woods.

Bruised or chopped leaves give off a faint garlic aroma, useful for flavouring salads and sauces. The leaves also make a good cooked vegetable. Add them to stews and casseroles.

Horseradish

Botanical name: *Armoracia rusticana* Family: *Cruciferae*

A perennial up to 1m (3ft) high with large, glossy, dock-like leaves. These give off the characteristic horseradish smell when crushed. In May and June white flowers appear on the tall, many-branched stem. Long woody roots rich in vitamin C used in same way as cultivated kind, but difficult to dig up. Not an indigenous wild herb but 'escapes' from gardens are common on waste ground, mostly in the south and Wales.

Use only the inner white part of the root; grate it for making into the traditional sauce. Warning: peeling is difficult and unpleasant, worse than onions!

Marjoram

Botanical name: *Origanum vulgare* Family: *Labiatae*

The most fragrant wild herb with a good spicy flavour for cooking. Pale mauve or pink flowers grow in clusters from July to September. Small oval leaves are smooth-edged. A native perennial found mainly in England and Wales on dry, scrubby places and hedgebanks, mostly on chalky soil.

Use leaves and flowers for flavouring and herb mixtures. Dries well for storing.

Meadowsweet

Botanical name: *Filipendula ulmaria* Family: *Rosaceae*

Perennial up to 1m (3ft) high. Square reddish stem, serrated leaves with downy silver undersides. Fragrant, creamy-white flowers grow in dense clusters from June to August. Widespread throughout Britain in wet places, marshy meadows, ditches, river banks.

Dried leaves of meadowsweet make an excellent flavouring herb, especially for drinks. Pour 575ml (1pt) boiling water over 25g (1oz) dried leaves. Allow to infuse 5 minutes before straining.

Mints

Botanical name: *Mentha arvensis*—field or corn mint
M. longifolia—horsemint
M. aquatica—watermint
M. pulegium—pennyroyal
Family: *Labiatae*

Field mint is a native perennial up to 50cm (1½ft) high, branched, rather hairy with pale green, oval, toothed leaves. From May to October lilac flowers form in the leaf axils, encircling the stalk, distinguishing it from other mints whose flowers grow in dense spikes. Common throughout Britain in arable fields, woods, waste ground and damp places.

Leaves strongly aromatic when picked before flowering. Use in place of garden mint.

Horsemint has pinky-mauve flowers on long stalks and white undersides to the leaves. The whole plant is hairy. Only locally common, mostly in damp places.

Watermint is a short perennial with thick hairy oval leaves in opposite pairs. From July to September it produces bushy heads of lilac flowers at the end of the stem and in top few leaf axils. Common in damp places everywhere.

Pennyroyal, once a favoured medicinal herb, now an uncommon mint with much smaller leaves and reddish, creeping, flowering stalks.

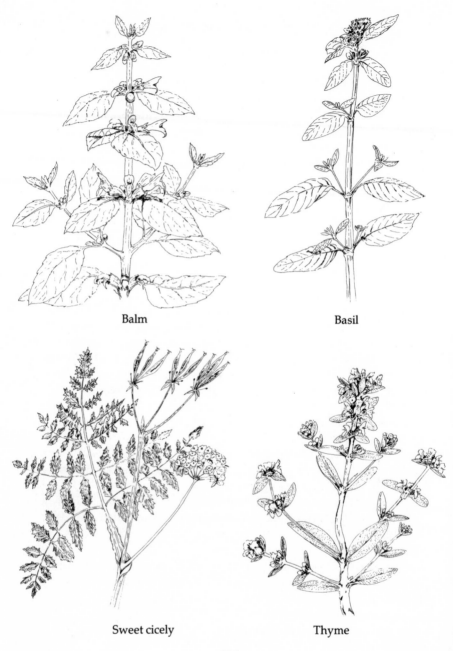

Balm

Basil

Sweet cicely

Thyme

Mugwort

Botanical name: *Artemisia vulgaris* Family: *Compositae*

Most artemisias are aromatic. Mugwort is a tall perennial with numerous cottony white flowerheads in leafy panicles, July–September. Bi-pinnate leaves are lobed, green above, woolly white beneath. Sturdy purplish stalks. Common in waste places, hedgerows and along roadsides.

Pick flower buds and use whole in small quantities in herb mixtures or to season fat meats, poultry and fish. Rub mugwort on the food before roasting. Dries well for storing.

Ramsons (wild garlic)

Botanical name: *Allium ursinum* Family: *Liliaceae*

A native bulb, the leaf resembles lily-of-the-valley. Whole plant has strong garlicky smell. Starlike white flowers bloom at the end of the long triangular stalks from April to June. Common in woods and damp places throughout England.

Two other garlic substitutes: field garlic (*Allium oleraceum*) and crow garlic (*A. vineale*), the latter more common in fields and along roadsides. These varieties look more like cultivated garlic, having long tubular stems, flat leaves and rosy flower heads consisting of clusters of bulbils from June onwards.

The strong garlic smell of ramsons fades considerably when cooked, so that chopped leaves added to savoury recipes will not overpower.

Sage (clary)

Botanical name: *Salvia verbenaca* Family: *Labiatae*

A common perennial, height to 65cm (2.2ft). Long spikes of purple flowers, each with two white spots on the lower lip. The large wrinkled hairy leaves are in pairs on the square brownish stem. Grows in dry fields and along roadsides, mostly in the south.

Use as substitute for garden sage in all recipes.

115

Sweet cicely

Botanical name: *Myrrhis odorata* Family: *Umbelliferae*

An early umbellifer, tall and attractive with hollow, furrowed stems, large, feathery leaves and white flower umbels May–June. Leaves turn purplish in autumn. Mostly a cultivated herb, sweet cicely grows wild in northern districts and Scotland in woods, hedges and grassy places.

A useful sweetening herb with anise aroma for adding to sour fruits and drinks. Leaves raw in salads, or to flavour soups and stews.

Thyme

Botanical name: *Thymus drucei* Family: *Labiatae*

Lovely little creeping perennial with sweet-smelling, pink flowers starting in May. Bees love it. The edges of the small leaves are hairy; also two opposite rows of hairs grow along the square, grooved stalks. Wild thyme is found on chalky heaths, banks and dry grassland throughout Britain, especially in the north.

Use this fragrant herb more lavishly than the garden variety. Dries well.

6

SEAWEEDS

Seaweed can play an important part in the British diet, both directly as a food and indirectly as manure and cattle food. This seems only natural, in an ecological sense, for a country with such an extensive coastline. Widespread on rocky shores, seaweed grows mostly between the tide marks and on the rocks just below the tide level. It is quite easy to collect with wading boots, since some of the plants are exposed at low water and others shelter in rock pools.

Seaweeds are algae and reproduce by spores. They are not flowering plants, though they have their seasons of growth. They have no roots but attach themselves to the rocks or stones by means of a powerful 'hold fast' which acts as a kind of suction pad. They get the nourishment they require from the surrounding water.

The edible seaweeds contain a high proportion of mineral salts, iodine, bromine, mannite (an odorous oil), bitter principles and volatile oils. Iodine is an important element in the maintenance of health, and seaweeds provide a valuable addition to the diet of those with glandular complaints. Once you are accustomed to the rather strong flavours, they add variety to meals and have a beneficial effect on the whole body.

Badderlocks (honey ware)

Botanical name: *Alaria esculenta* Family: *Algae*

Badderlocks is a common seaweed with long, yellow-green, ribbon-like fronds which grow over 60cm (2ft) long. Growing out of the longish stems just below the frond are the keys, little finger-like

117

fronds. The stems are very pliable and with the aid of the fingers the seaweed is able to withstand the violent wave action to which it is often subjected. The stem extends the whole length of the fronds like a midrib.

Badderlocks, like other seaweeds, is full of iodine and other mineral elements so has plenty of nutriment. Growing on submerged rocks, it is most commonly found around the northern coasts of mainland Scotland and the islands. Badderlocks can be collected all the year round, but is at its most succulent from March to May.

USES

It is the midrib stem and 'fingers' growing around the stalk which are the parts of badderlocks to be eaten raw. The rind is stripped from the stem and the sweet-tasting inner portion is cut into bite-sized pieces and covered in vinegar. Serve as a pickle with meats.

Badderlocks in butter sauce
Remove the stems of the badderlocks and wash them thoroughly in cold water. Cut the stems into short lengths and tie in small bundles. Put into cold water or water and milk and bring slowly to the boil. Simmer over a low heat until tender. Serve with butter sauce.

Bladderwrack (cutweed, sea-wrack)

Botanical name: *Fucus vesiculosis* Family: *Fucaceae*

Bladderwrack consists of long, brownish-yellow fronds which attach themselves to the rocks by means of an effective disc-shaped 'holdfast'. All the nourishment the plant requires is taken in through the fronds from the surrounding sea water. The fronds are divided into flat, tough strips each of which has a strong midrib. At intervals along either side of the midrib there are globular swellings which are lined with mucus. These air pockets can be up to half an inch long and give the plant its characteristic name. The knobbed ends of the fronds contain the spore-producing structure by which the seaweed reproduces itself.

Bladderwrack contains health-giving mineral salts which include iodine, sodium and potassium. Growing in abundance, bladderwrack can be found at the half-tide mark and on partly submerged

Bladderwrack

rocks along the shores. Gather the seaweed by cutting the fronds of the living plant at least 15cm (6ins) away from the 'holdfast'. The best time for cutting is early to middle summer when the plant is at its best.

Seaweed thrown up onto the shore by the sea is best left alone because the detached plants quickly lose their properties.

USES

Preserve bladderwrack by drying it as rapidly as possible in the sun. It will then grind down to a coarse powder which can be stored in a screwtop jar. This can be added to soups and stews for extra nutrition. Bladderwrack can be cooked and eaten as a plain vegetable with a knob of butter added just before serving.

Creamed bladderwrack
Wash the fresh fronds thoroughly, put them into boiling water and

119

simmer until tender. Chop the fronds finely. Have ready a thick white sauce and add to the bladderwrack.

Mix well together and serve hot.

Carragheen (Irish moss, Dorset moss)

Botanical name: *Chondrus crispus* Family: *Algae*

The green or reddish-purple fronds of the carragheen moss are a familiar sight along the western and southern shores of Britain. The fronds are very deeply divided, tough and almost translucent. The stems are flat and branch out at the top into a fan shape, the segments of which can vary considerably in width. Irish moss is the name given to dried bleached carragheen.

Carragheen contains sulphur compounds together with a large amount of mucilage. This provides an important vegetable gelatine which is extremely nourishing. Carragheen can be found at low tide, growing in plenty in Ireland and on the shores of the Channel Islands as well as along the rocky coasts of south-west England. The

Carragheen

best time to gather carragheen is in April and May whilst it is young, when it will be a light brown colour.

It should be used either when quite fresh or carefully dried and stored for winter use. Dry the seaweed naturally by first washing it very thoroughly in plenty of fresh water to get rid of the salt and sand. Lay it outside to dry and bleach. When bleached white, remove the stems and bring it indoors to dry completely. Store in airtight jars.

USES

Use dried carragheen to thicken soups, stews and sauces and as a setting agent in place of the commercial gelatine in blancmanges, fruit jellies, aspics and custards. When carragheen is added to hot milk or water, it forms a gelatinous paste which must be strained before using. Caragheen jellies are cloudy but very nutritious.

Carragheen mould

Soak 12g (½oz) prepared carragheen in water to cover for 10 minutes. Drain off the water. Pour 850ml (1½pt) milk onto the carragheen, add three heaped tablespoons sugar and the rind of a lemon or a bay leaf. Bring slowly to the boil and simmer for 25–30 minutes. Strain and cool slightly. Whip up 150ml (¼pt) double cream and combine with the carragheen mixture. Heat to just under boiling point. Pour into a wetted mould and leave to set.

Turn out the mould and serve with fresh fruit.

Dulse (dillisk)

Botanical name: *Rhodymenia palmata* Family: *Rhodymeniaceae*

A pleasant edible sea weed, dulse tastes rather like oysters. The bright red fronds are fan-shaped, flat and deeply divided. It clings steadfastly to stones and rocks. One of the most common seaweeds, it is extremely nutritious and a good source of vegetable protein, containing a high concentration of the mineral salts iodine and bromine.

Dulse is found growing on the middle and lower shores round Britain. It can be gathered all the year round but is at its best in early spring and summer.

121

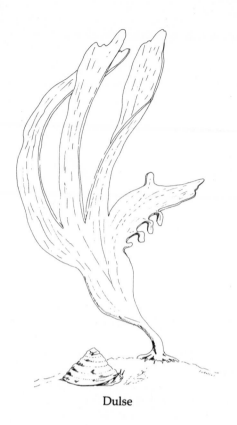

Dulse

Dulse can be eaten raw in salads or the dried fronds can be fried, crumbled and added to vegetable or fish soups. The fronds are rather tough, and to prepare dulse as a vegetable it must first be well washed in plenty of fresh water and then soaked for three hours in cold water.

Savoury dulse
Cover soaked dulse with milk, add a lump of butter, pepper and salt and simmer covered for 3 or 4 hours until tender and the liquid is absorbed. Cut the dulse into small pieces and serve on fingers of brown-bread toast. Alternatively, mix chopped dulse with mashed potato and chopped parsley, adding enough hot milk to make it creamy and smooth. It goes well with meat or fish dishes.

Kelp (sea-girdles, tangle)

Botanical name: *Laminaria digitata*
Laminaria stenophylla
Laminaria saccharina
Family: *Laminariaceae*

Kelp is dried seaweed and, in particular, is the name given to those large seaweeds, the laminaria, which are collected, dried and burnt. Iodine, carbonate of soda and charcoal were all obtained from the ashes and these were formerly used for making soap, glass and medicines. Three tons of laminaria end up as one ton of kelp, and each ton can yield as much as 5½kg (12lb) of iodine. A good source of alginates, the laminarias are used as vegetable gelatines. The large, browny-yellow fronds are flat and very deeply indented. They grow up to 30cm (12in) across and on strong stems 5–25cm (2–10in) long. The whole seaweed reaches a length of 1.5–1.8m (5–6ft).

Laminaria saccharina is known as 'poor man's weatherglass'. *Laminaria digitata* is full of minerals and contains nearly ten times as much iodine as bladderwrack. The laminarias are found growing only at the low-tide mark on rocky, sandy shores all round the coasts of Britain. *Laminaria digitata* is a deep-water seaweed and must be gathered as 'driftwood kelp' when thrown up on the shore. Where possible, gather the kelp in May and June when at its best, though it can be collected all the year round.

USES

The tender stalks of the young fronds can be eaten raw, well washed, then chopped finely and added to salads. Kelp makes an excellent food supplement with its high nutriment value, and the dried, powdered seaweed can be sprinkled onto soups and meat casseroles.

Alternatively, it can be used as a thickening agent in cooking savoury dishes.

Kelp patties

Wash freshly gathered laminaria in plenty of cold water to remove all sand. Place in a saucepan with milk, seasoning and a knob of butter. Cover and cook over gentle heat or in a low oven until tender. This can take up to 3 hours. Drain off milk, cool and mince the kelp. Mix with chopped onions, tomatoes and cooked bacon. Add flour to make a drier mixture, form into flat cakes and fry lightly in oil.

Laver (sea spinach, purple laver)

Botanical name: *Porphyra umbilicalis*
Porphyra laciniata
Family: *Algae*

A widespread and well-known seaweed, laver is easy to recognise with its large purple fronds crinkled and cut in irregular notches. The fronds are very thin and membranous, covering rocks with a rather slimy film. All species of porphyra are called laver in England and Wales—this is the 'sloke' of Ireland. A very popular seaweed in Japan, the laver (*Porphyra vulgaris*) is cultivated on a large scale. In early spring, branches of oak are laid in the shallow water of the bay near Tokyo. Laver quickly appears on these branches and is harvested from October to March, to be sold in the markets.

Laver contains a high proportion of iodine as well as the vitamins C and P (Hesperedin) and other mineral elements. Laver grows in abundance on rocky, stony shores all round Britain but especially on the west coast. It grows at all levels of the tide on open beaches.

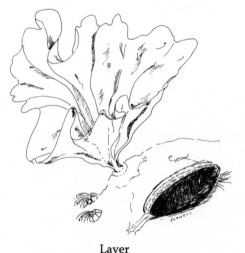

Laver

124

The best month for collecting laver is March, but it can be gathered from June to March.

USES
Laver is a well-known delicacy in Wales, and is first made into laver-bread which forms the basis for other dishes. The traditional sauce eaten with Welsh mutton is made from laver-bread; it is also used for hors d'oeuvre and savouries. Wash the laver in plenty of fresh water to remove the sand. Put into a pan with water to cover and bring slowly to the boil. Simmer it gently until quite tender. Strain off the water and add a little salt, beat to a purée or put through an electric blender.

Keep the purée in jars in the refrigerator.

Laver hors d'oeuvre

Mix some laver prepared as above, together with a little olive oil, lemon juice, pepper and salt. Do not let the mixture become too moist.

Chill in the refrigerator and serve cold on toast.

Sea lettuce (green laver)

Botanical name: *Ulva lactuca* Family: *Algae*

The irregular, wavy-edged, translucent, flat and very thin fronds of sea lettuce are a lovely light-green colour and grow in clusters up to 45cm (18in) high. Very similar to laver, sea lettuce has less flavour and is not so tender, but can be used in the same ways. It is rather like spinach but has an oyster-like flavour.

Very nutritious, sea lettuce contains iodine and many other mineral elements. It grows in profusion where fresh water meets the sea and in pools high on the shoreline in summer. In winter it grows at the mid-tide mark. It attaches itself to rock and stones wherever it can and is mainly found on the shores of Wales, Cornwall and Devon.

Gather sea lettuce any time between the months of June and March, but the flavour is more pronounced when collected in March.

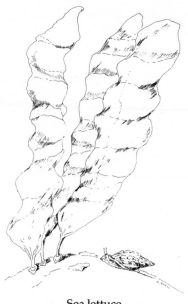

Sea lettuce

Sea lettuce is prepared and cooked in the same ways as laver. Always wash the seaweed thoroughly in several lots of cold water before cooking it slowly over gentle heat for 3–4 hours.

Sea-lettuce rolls
Cook the sea lettuce as suggested above. Mix with fine oatmeal or wholemeal flour to bind it together. Form into small rolls and fry in bacon fat. Serve with bacon and eggs for breakfast.

7

MUSHROOMS AND OTHER FUNGI

Wild mushrooms, fungi and nuts, the 'meats' of the wild larder, can provide valuable, free, nutritious foods to enrich the diet. In addition to their content of vegetable protein, unsaturated fat and carbohydrates, they are rich in vitamins and minerals, and can be eaten raw or cooked in every kind of dish. These foods are especially valuable for vegetarians.

With a little instruction and the study of a good field guide it is easy to learn to identify the many hundred or so wild grassland mushrooms and woodland fungi that are worth eating. Truffles, prized underground tubers once collected in English woods with the help of trained dogs, are rarely found today. The few really poisonous fungi are not difficult to recognise; see the list on pages 10–11. The varieties to use with caution, such as fairy-ring champignon and the edible russula fungi, not included in the following details of individual species, should only be collected after careful study or confirmation by a specialist.

Follow these basic rules for fungi collecting and using:

1 Gather only young, whole fungi well known to you, unless you are accompanied by an experienced collector. It is useful to keep a diary of species gathered, noting habitats and time of year.

2 Twist fungi carefully from the ground complete with base of stem to identify the dangerous amanita, and to preserve next year's crop.

3 Clean off dirt from fungi immediately, and shorten stem a little to check for insect damage.

4 Never wash fungi unless they can be prepared and cooked straight away. Follow the directions given for each variety. Dry, or preserve by other methods previously described, any sound specimens that cannot be used soon after collection. Dried fungi can be reconstituted by soaking in water, then using in the same way as fresh mushrooms in the recipes.

5 Never eat too many mushrooms in a meal.

Anise cap

Botanical name: *Clitocybe odora* Family: *Tricholomataceae*

The anise cap is a small, aromatic fungus with a blue-green or greeny-grey coloured cap 3–10cm (1–4in) across. When young it is convex in shape, but as it matures the cap flattens and becomes concave with rather wavy edges. The gills and stem are white, tinged with green.

In autumn anise caps can be found in damp coniferous woods, especially under pine trees. The strong aniseed scent helps you to discover them growing among the rotting needles.

USES
An excellent variety to mix with less aromatic mushrooms; use anise caps to flavour soups, stews, casseroles, in sauces and stuffings. Always use freshly picked caps as their fragrance fades when dried.

Anise-cap stuffing
Chop cleaned and trimmed anise-cap fungi into small pieces. Heat oil in a pan and gently sauté the pieces together with sliced spring onions until soft. Mix with chopped or minced parsley, marjoram, lemon balm and thyme. Add a little vegetable stock, a beaten egg and breadcrumbs to make a firm mixture. Use in stuffed Good King Henry leaves.

Anise cap with spinach

225g (8oz) anise cap
900g (2lb) spinach
50g (2oz) grated cheese
125ml (4floz) fresh cream
75g (3oz) butter

25g (1oz) flour
1 egg
1 teacupful milk
seasoning

128

Wash spinach well and cook in boiling salted water. Drain, refresh in cold water and drain again. Chop spinach finely and mix with 50g (2oz) of butter. Clean anise caps, discarding stems. Blanch in boiling salted water for 10 minutes. Drain and chop caps into small pieces.

Make a white sauce with remaining 25g (1oz) butter, flour and milk, season to taste. Add anise caps, mix together and fold in half the cream. Lay half the spinach on the bottom of an ovenproof dish, cover with anise-cap filling, and place remaining spinach on top. Beat the egg with the rest of the cream and pour over spinach.

Place in hot oven 200°C (400°F, Gas 6) until golden brown. Serve at once.

Blewits

Botanical name: *Tricholoma personatum*—blueleg
Tricholoma nudum—wood blewit or bluecap
Family: *Tricholomataceae*

The fleshy cap of the blueleg blewit is greyish-brown, sometimes tinged lilac or purple. When young, the cap is rounded but it becomes convex and later flattened; it may be 7–15cm (3–6in) wide. The short, stout stem, slightly swollen at the base, is whitish and covered with lilac-coloured fibrils. The similar coloured gills are broad and crowded. The flesh of bluelegs is a grey colour when damp but white when dry.

The wood blewit or bluecap, a smaller, less fleshy mushroom, is entirely blue or a beautiful amethyst purple. The colour fades gradually to a cloudy purple. In deciduous woods bluecaps tend to be a brownish colour, whereas in coniferous woods they are a bright purple. The cap has a wavy margin; the stem may be attached to the base of another specimen, to fallen leaves or coniferous needles.

Bluelegs may be found in forests of all kinds, meadows, pastures, on downs and in well-manured apple orchards beneath the trees. They often grow in large circles or rows where the grass is darker than the surrounding growth. They usually appear from September to November and are still edible after the first frost. Best gathered in dry weather. Bluecaps grow in groups or rings in, or near, woods, orchards and parks or on compost heaps. Gather on dry days from mid-October to December.

129

Blewits are tender, fragile and rather watery. They smell faintly of radishes. Stew in butter or oil, or add to other vegetable stews and serve in a white sauce. Blewits produce their own liquid when stewing. Add them to hot fat in a skillet in which chopped onions have been softened. Cook quickly until tender in a covered pan. If liquid is needed, add a little stock or white wine.

To preserve, either dry or powder them. Bottle in brine or pickle in vinegar. Blewits are suitable for mushroom relish (see recipe page 137).

Blewit stew
Remove the stems from the caps and chop them finely. Put the caps into a shallow casserole dish and pack them round with the chopped stems and an equal amount of finely chopped onion. Add a little butter and one or two sage leaves. Cover and cook slowly over a low heat for half an hour. Drain off the liquid and use it to make a sauce with butter and flour. Simmer until thick then pour over the blewit caps. Re-cover the dish and cook for a further half-hour.

Serve with roast meat.

Blewits in sauce

275ml (10floz) good white sauce	parsley
50g (2oz) blewits	salt and paprika
1 small onion, finely chopped	

Trim and slice blewits, fold in white sauce with the onion, parsley and seasoning to taste. Simmer, covered, for 10–15 minutes, stirring occasionally.

Serve on toast or with boiled chicken.

Ceps

Botanical name: *Boletus edulis*
Boletus aestivalis
Family: *Boletaceae*

Ceps is the English name for the most common and popular fungi belonging to the large group of boleti to be found in this country.

Ceps

They are fleshy, shaped rather like mushrooms but more colourful. Instead of gills they have a layer of vertical tubes, the open ends of which appear as fine pores, like a sponge. Study the field guide carefully for identification in order to distinguish between the edible, of which there are about 70 indigenous species, and the many non-edible boleti.

The fully grown cap of ceps is 5–20cm (2–8in) across. Smooth and moist to the touch it is a warm chestnut-brown fading to a paler shade or almost white at the outer edges. When it first appears, the cap is small and round, hardly wider than its swollen, finely veined stem. The short, narrow tubes barely reach the stem which, when fully grown, varies in length from 5–15cm (2–6in). Stem and tubes start white, then turn yellowish and finish a yellowy-green colour. The flesh of ceps is always white, thick and firm, often pinkish under the cuticle, but never changes colour when broken.

Boletus aestivalis is very similar to *Boletus edulis* and just as good to eat. Its cap is greyish ochre to pale brown with a light-brown leathery stem covered in a network of veins. (See also Chapter 9 for other edible boleti.)

Ceps are a valuable wild food, a good source of protein, fat and minerals. They also contain vitamin D, not found in other vegetables.

131

Ceps are found in the undergrowth of spruce forests, as well as in beechwoods; they also grow amongst heather and along forest paths and boundaries, usually on acid soil. Gather ceps from June to October.

USES
Ceps have a pleasant, mushroomy aroma and a mild sweet taste, like nut kernels. They can be cooked in a great variety of ways, or used raw in salads. They need careful preparation (see pages 26–8), as their tubes should be removed if they are soft. The stems, if free of maggots which attack them in dry spells, may also be used. Separate them from the caps, scrape and cut into slices. Put into a baking dish fried ceps slices mixed with slices of cooked potato or wild edible roots and chopped chives. Mix together one egg, a little milk and a tablespoon of flour smoothed with a cup of yoghurt or sour cream. Pour sauce over the ceps and bake in a low oven 140°C (275°F, Gas 1) until set.

Egged and breadcrumbed
Cut long thick slices of ceps first seasoned with salt and dipped in flour, then in egg and breadcrumbs. Fry in hot oil or other fat.

Au gratin
Add cooked ceps slices and chopped hard-boiled egg to a cream sauce, sprinkle with grated cheese and brown in a hot oven 220°C (425°F, Gas 7). Or top with breadcrumbs and chopped fennel leaves and dot with butter.

Fried in batter
Serve with garlic-flavoured mayonnaise.

Grilled
Marinate cleaned ceps and stalks in a mixture of oil seasoned with salt and paprika for 2–3 hours. Then grill and serve with a little of the marinade oil in which garlic, chives and parsley are quickly cooked, adding a dash of lemon juice.

Stuffed
Use caps (all dry varieties) well flavoured with herbs and seasoning.

In salads
Raw: trim and rinse under tap. Drain and cut in fine slices, dress with salad dressing of your choice. Cooked: first stew slices of ceps gently in a little oil until tender. Or scald in boiling water, drain and allow to cool. Dress with lemon juice flavoured with salad herbs, or marinate cooked slices in oil and lemon juice for half an hour.

Spread
Stew finely chopped boleti in butter or margarine until quite soft. Pass through a sieve or purée in an electric blender. Mix with cream cheese, thin with cream if necessary and season well. Or use scalded slices and add chopped onions and herbs. Serve spread on toast, wholemeal bread or biscuits.

In soups
Mince or chop 350g (12oz) of a single variety of boletus or a mixture. Heat oil in a skillet and fry till golden 2 tablespoons chopped onions or leeks. Add minced mushrooms and cook till tender. Sprinkle with 2 tablespoons flour or fine breadcrumbs, then add 1½l (2½pt) good stock. Season and bring to boil. Simmer for half an hour. Serve sprinkled with parsley. Vary the seasonings—try a pinch of curry powder just before serving and sprinkle with chopped celery leaves.

In sauces
Add finely chopped cooked ceps to white or brown sauces.

Minced
Trim and clean but do not wash, then chop up ceps or other fungi finely. In hot fat, gently fry chopped onions, parsley, chives, spring onions and a mixture of herbs or any wild flavouring herbs in season. Add and fry the mushrooms until liquid has evaporated. Soak an equal quantity of stale bread in hot water until soft, squeeze out well and add to mixture in pan. Continue cooking over low heat until well mixed in and dry. Cool slightly, add one egg and season with salt, nutmeg and ground ginger. Use mixture for rissoles, savoury cakes, dumplings and stuffings.

En casserole

Use ceps only. Season centre of cap with salt, paprika, a sprinkling of lemon juice and a dab of butter. Add softened onion slices if liked. Cover casserole with lid and cook in a medium oven 180°C (350°F, Gas 4) for 20–40 minutes till tender. Serve on toast, with vegetables or rice. Garnish with chopped parsley, chives or other mild herbs. Or add breadcrumbs and sour cream or cheese before finishing, and serve from the casserole.

In mixed stew

Make this from a mixture of collected edible fungi and mushrooms. Chop and fry some onion, garlic, parsley and chives and other herbs in hot butter or fat. Add the seasoned fungi, leaving small ones whole and chopping others. Cook covered for 10 minutes. Add stock if too dry and any cubed cooked vegetables to hand. This mixture can also be crisped in the oven, adding some sour cream on top before browning.

All boleti are good for preserving. Ceps are best dried or powdered but should be cut into very thin strips before stringing and drying. They may also be frozen or pickled in vinegar or brine.

Cèpes en Provence

Trim and wash 450g (1lb) ceps. Cut about ¾ of them into thick slices and chop the remainder finely. Heat oil in a skillet and cook the ceps slices for 10–15 minutes, turning once. Add chopped ceps, 2 onions and 1 clove of garlic, finely chopped. Continue cooking until tender, stirring continuously. Season and add 2 tablespoons chopped parsley and the juice of half a lemon.

Serve on a bed of hot mashed potatoes or other cooked vegetable, or as a vegetable on their own.

Beef marrow with ceps

4 ceps	marrow from 3 beef bones
2 shallots	previously cooked in stock
60g (2½oz) butter	seasoning

Clean firm young ceps, and remove the stalks. Mince stalks with shallots and sauté in half the butter over gentle heat. Add bone marrow. Put cep caps into buttered dish in a hot oven, 200°C (400°F,

Gas 6), for 10 minutes to soften. Place the mince on the caps and dot with remaining butter. Heat through in the oven for 15 minutes. Serve hot on toast.

Chanterelles

Botanical name: *Cantherellus cibarius*—chanterelle, egg sponge
Cantharellus infundibuliformis
Craterellus cornucopioides—horn of plenty
Family: *Cantharellaceae*

The chanterelle is so easy to recognise by its egg-yolk colour and unusual shape that children can collect it without risk. Chanterelles have a distinctive cap approximately 3–10cm (1–4in) across, lobed and convex when young, becoming funnel-shaped with elevated, thick, wavy margins. The thick, rounded gills are very shallow and extend down the stem in folds. Fully grown, the stem only reaches a height of 5cm (2in), narrowing at the base. When young it is almost as wide as the cap, and being the same bright-yellow colour it is often difficult to see where stalk begins and cap ends. The thick brittle flesh of chanterelles is tinted yellow but is creamy-coloured when dry.

Chanterelles

135

Chanterelles are nutritious mushrooms, valuable for their high content of vitamin A as well as other vitamins, protein, fats, and minerals.

Cantharellus infundibuliformis is another edible variety of chanterelle, with a dark brown cap and wavy, crisped margins. The stem is long, grooved and deep yellow in colour. The flesh is aromatic but inclined to be tough and somewhat bitter. The horn of plenty is closely related to chanterelles and is also edible. It is similar in shape but cap and stem are a dark dingy brown, grey or black.

Chanterelles are found from summer to autumn in all kinds of woods, often in moss, and in damp, sunny places and clearings.

Cantharellus infundibuliformis grows in deciduous and coniferous woods on acid soil. Horn of plenty is found from August to November clustered under beech trees and among dead leaves of other deciduous trees.

USES

Chanterelles give a special tang to egg and vegetable dishes and can be used raw or cooked in salads. Best fried or stewed and added to soups, sauces, meat stews; or chop and use them in stuffings. They are delicious fried and eaten with scrambled eggs, or in a mixed mushroom stew consisting of chanterelles, morels and boleti. Do not bake chanterelles in the oven as slow cooking makes them tough.

Use only young, sound specimens and be sure to discard the over-ripe or sodden ones as these may cause indigestion.

Chanterelles transport well and will keep fresh in the fridge or a cool place for several days. They dry well and may also be frozen, bottled, pickled or made into relish and sauces.

Horn of plenty has a good mushroomy flavour in spite of its tougher texture. Boiled or fried it will season any savoury recipe requiring mushrooms. Slice and fry in batter, or use horn of plenty as an omelette filling. Horn of plenty is one of the best fungi for preserving, especially by drying when it becomes more intensely aromatic.

Chanterelles and tomatoes

Fry a chopped onion in hot oil or fat until soft. Add 4 large tomatoes cut in thin slices and 450g (1lb) of chanterelles, trimmed, washed and quartered. Continue cooking for 10 minutes. Season and sprinkle the vegetables with a little flour, add 1 tablespoon lemon juice and 3 tablespoons thin cream. If the mixture is too dry a little vegetable stock may also be added. Cook a further 5 minutes or until fungi are tender.

Serve sprinkled with parsley and a pinch of basil.

Relish
Use fully developed chanterelles and any edible mushrooms. Break them into pieces, put in a bowl and sprinkle over them about 50g (2oz) of salt to each 450g (1lb) of mushrooms. Leave them for 3–4 days, stirring at least once each day.

Transfer mushrooms to fireproof dish, place it in a slow oven and cook the mushrooms gently for approximately 1 hour. Strain off liquor and to each 2.2l (quart) of liquid add 1 teaspoon each of whole allspice, dried root ginger and peppercorns, a few cloves and ½ teaspoon each cinnamon and spice. If using ground spices, add one-quarter of these quantities during the original cooking. A small onion and mixed herbs may also be added with the spices. Boil the spiced liquor until it is reduced by half.

Strain the relish while still hot into warm bottles and seal at once.

Chanterelles and rice patties

225g (8oz) chanterelles	50g (2oz) butter or margarine
200g (7oz) rice	5 tablespoons grated cheese
750ml (1½pt) light stock	seasoning

Prepare chanterelles, sauté lightly in a little fat. Drain and chop them up into small pieces. Wash rice and simmer gently in stock until cooked. Drain and mix with softened butter and grated cheese. Into small greased moulds put layers of rice mixture and chanterelles. Cover the moulds and cook in a hot oven, 200°C (400°F, Gas 6), for 20–30 minutes.

Field or common mushroom

Botanical name: *Agaricus (psalliota) campestris*
Agaricus (psalliota) arvensis—horse mushroom
Family: *Agaricaceae*

The field mushroom resembles the cultivated mushroom but has more flavour. The cap starts as a white silky ball, then becomes convex and finally flat, varying in size from 5–12cm (2–5in). The firm, tapering stem always has a thin, white, torn ring; on young specimens the ring stands out from the stem but later hangs down and eventually shrivels and falls away. The gills of field mushrooms are thin, crowded and free from the stem; they start a deep-pink colour, becoming darker, and finally turn a purplish-brown or

Field mushroom

Amanita muscaria—highly poisonous

black. The flesh is white and soft, but changes to a reddish or dirty brown if broken or cut.

Horse mushrooms are much larger than field mushrooms. The cap starts white but turns a browny-yellow with age or bruising, and may reach a width of 15–20cm (6–8in). The tall, thick stem carries a broader ring, described as a 'double' structure, having a second outer and lower membrane. The gills of the horse mushroom are always a greyish colour and never a deep pink like the field mushroom, but they turn brown or black with age and remain dry. The flesh is pure white and becomes bright yellow when bruised or cut, when it also gives off its characteristic aroma of almonds. Some other edible agarics are: *Agaricus silvicola*—wood mushroom, very similar to horse mushroom; *Agaricus silvaticus; A. langei, A. augustus, A. bitorquis* and *A. subperonatus.*

Warning: Correct identification of field and horse mushrooms is important to avoid confusing them with the following:

1 Yellow stainer (*Agaricus xanthodermus*). Very similar in appearance to horse mushroom but cap stains bright yellow on rubbing or bruising and at swollen base of stem on cutting. Unpleasant carbolic smell. Not poisonous but avoid.

2 Fly agaric (*Amanita muscaria*). Dangerously poisonous, the 'fairy' toadstool with bright red and white spotted cap.

3 Death cap (*Amanita phalloides*). DEADLY. Olive-yellow cap, white gills.

4 Destroying angel (*Amanita virosa*). DEADLY. Entirely white, easily mistaken for field mushroom.

5 Panther cap (*Amanita pantherina*). DEADLY. Smoky brown cap with white warts.

6 Fool's mushroom (*Amanita verna*). DEADLY. Resembles destroying angel, above.

7 False death cap (*Amanita citrina* or *mappa*). The double of the real death cap. There is also a white variety. Neither is poisonous but can be mistaken for destroying angel and death cap so are best avoided.

Always dig up suspect mushrooms to examine stem and base. Cut base of stem to check for yellow staining. The really poisonous fungi have a ring and bulbous base encased in a 'volva'. This resembles a thick cup with loose edges, half free from the stem. In their early stages these fungi are completely covered by the unbroken volva called a 'universal veil'. Volva and gills are always white. Edible agaric mushrooms have no volva and the gills are grey or pink to chocolate colour.

Field mushrooms can be found in meadows and fields and on downs where animals have grazed. Also in gardens and on paths away from trees. In dry seasons they often grow in abundance, sometimes forming irregular rings from early summer to autumn. They are best picked in dry conditions as they deteriorate quickly when wet.

Horse mushrooms may be found from July to October in open fields, sometimes near hay and straw stacks, and in spruce forests.

USES

The flavour of field mushrooms is pleasant and mild. The scent is only faint, unlike its cousin the horse mushroom, which has a much stronger flavour and smells of almonds. Some people compare it with aniseed.

Both mushrooms can be cooked in the same ways and in any mushroom recipe. Young specimens need no peeling, but make sure they are free of maggots by cutting in half or trimming away the tip of the stem. Clean caps by wiping over with a damp cloth, or brush off any earth and grass with a pastry brush.

Field and horse mushrooms are good on toast, with eggs and bacon or a mixed grill, raw or cooked in salads, and as a vegetable on their own. They flavour and fill out stews and casseroles, make delicious soups and can be fried in batter, added to stuffings or used in soufflés and au gratin dishes. The larger caps are good stuffed. Choose small caps for adding to salads and to sauté in butter or bacon fat. Do not over cook them as they take only a few minutes; any longer and they become mushy, yet tough.

Additions of any of the following will bring out the flavour of mushrooms: onions and garlic (very little), lemon juice, sour cream and tomatoes. Herbs and spices that blend well: rosemary, sage, summer savory, basil, tarragon, lemon balm, cloves and nutmeg. Or make up a quantity of the following herbs to sprinkle over cooked mushrooms as required: 2 tablespoons each of parsley and dill; 1 tablespoon each chives, celery leaves, tarragon.

Field and horse mushrooms are suitable for drying and freezing or they may be bottled. Cook small caps with stems in a little butter and lemon juice for a few minutes. Drain and pack into jars. Cover with home-made tomato pulp seasoned with herbs, salt, paprika and a pinch of sugar. Use the older, dark-coloured mushrooms for making relish or ketchup (see recipe page 137).

Mushroom soufflé

350g (¾lb) chopped field mushrooms	bechamel sauce: made from 25g (2oz) butter, 12g (½oz) flour, 150ml (5floz) milk
butter	
1 tablespoon finely chopped onion	4 egg yolks
pinch paprika	5 egg whites
grated cheese	

Melt butter in a pan and gently sauté mushrooms with onion and paprika until soft. Allow to cool. Melt butter for sauce in a pan, stir in flour until smooth. Gradually add the milk and stir until boiling. Cool slightly, then beat in the egg yolks one at a time, adding seasoning to taste. Whip egg whites to a firm snow and fold quickly into the sauce.

Have ready a buttered soufflé dish and cover the bottom with the mixture. Layer with half the mushrooms, more soufflé mixture then remaining mushrooms. Cover with soufflé mixture and sprinkle cheese and browned breadcrumbs on top. Bake in a moderate oven 180°C (350°F, Gas 3) for 25–30 minutes until well risen and firm.

Serve at once.

Stuffed mushrooms

Use large unblemished caps. Remove stems, chop and sauté them together with some chopped fungi in 1 tablespoon butter until soft. Sieve or purée the fungi, add breadcrumbs, chopped hazelnuts, some chopped chives, a little tarragon or wild ramsons and basil. Bind the mixture with cream, stock or sherry. Season with salt and paprika. Brush caps with melted butter or oil and place in a flat, buttered, fireproof dish. Fill caps with the *farce* and sprinkle with grated parmesan or other strong cheese. Bake in low oven 170°C (325°F, Gas 3), for 20 minutes. Alternatively, put the stuffed caps in a greased pan and grill for about 5 minutes. Serve very hot on toast or creamed spinach. Stuffing may also be made with a simple *farce* made of cooked puréed mushrooms, or with seafood for a party starter.

Horse mushroom rolls

Put horse mushrooms into a pan, cover with milk and add a pinch of powdered mace. Cook until soft. Drain and finely chop the mushrooms. When cold mix the mushrooms with half their amount in chopped ham and sufficient thick white sauce to bind them together. Roll out short crust or puff pastry thinly and spread the mushroom mixture on top. Roll the pastry up lengthwise to look like a swiss roll. Cut the roll into slices and lay them flat on a baking tray. Brush with beaten egg and cook them in a hot oven 220°C (425°F, Gas 7) for 7–10 minutes. Eat hot.

Horse mushroom tart

450g (1lb) horse mushrooms	juice of half a small lemon
225g (8oz) shortcrust pastry	275ml (10floz) milk
50g (2oz) butter	pinch of cayenne
25g (1oz) flour	seasoning

Roll out pastry, line an 8-inch flan ring and bake blind in hot oven 200°C (400°F, Gas 6), for 10–15 minutes. Clean mushrooms with care and cook in a covered pan with 25g (1oz) butter, lemon juice and seasoning. With the remaining butter, flour and milk make a creamy white sauce. Add this to mushrooms with a pinch of cayenne, and stir well.

Pour mixture into pastry case and serve hot or cold.

Mushroom-stuffed tomatoes

4 large tomatoes	2 tablespoons butter
225g (8oz) mushrooms, minced or chopped small	275ml (10floz) stock
½ clove of garlic, crushed	2 tablespoons breadcrumbs
	seasoning

Cut a lid from the flower end of the tomatoes and scoop out the inside with a small spoon. In a pan, cook together the tomato pulp, minced mushrooms and garlic in one tablespoon of butter and 150ml (5floz) stock for about 15 minutes. Season and fill tomatoes with the mixture. Place the tomatoes on a baking pan, sprinkle with breadcrumbs, dot with remaining butter and pour in remaining stock.

Bake in a medium oven, 180°C (350°F, Gas 4), for 15 minutes.

Honey fungus

Botanical name: *Armillaria mellea* Family: *Agaricaceae*

One of Britain's commonest edible fungi, honey fungus is a very destructive parasite. It attacks live and dead trees, its thread-like spores spreading rapidly underground. The tufted caps of honey fungus, usually yellowish brown, the colour of honey, are 5–15cm (2–6in) wide and covered in tiny, dark, fibrous scales. The gills extend a short way down the stem, their colour a dirty white tinged with pink to start, turning to pale brownish-yellow, sometimes spotted brown. The thick, yellow-flecked stem is approximately 5–20cm (2–8in) tall, bulbous at the base and tufted below the yellow volval ring.

Honey fungi are found in groups of up to twenty growing together from one stem on dead and living trees of all kinds and on old stumps and roots. It is possible to find very large solitary specimens but this is more rare. September is the time when honey fungi are most plentiful, but they can appear as early as June. Be sure to identify them correctly and not confuse them with other fungi which grow in the same manner and habitats. Two of these species are *Pholiota squarrosa*, recognisable by the sharp scales covering cap, ring and stem; and the poisonous sulphur tuft, *Hypholoma fasciculare*, with its bright sulphur-yellow colour. Sulphur tuft fungi look like a non-poisonous but unpleasant cousin, *Hypholoma sublateritium*, which is browner and has a whitish stem.

USES

The flavour of honey fungus is strong and spicy—some consider it bitter—and its popularity varies from region to region. The young fruit bodies may be collected whole, but only the caps of the older ones are worth eating. Honey fungi are excellent for flavouring casseroles and other mushroom dishes, especially for chopping or blending to provide a flavour and ingredient for stuffings. If sautéing or stewing always cook them uncovered, as the somewhat acidy

143

smell then disappears, changing to a pleasant mushroomy aroma.

Honey fungus is a good variety for drying to provide flavouring. Use the big caps for this—check for maggots and make sure the caps are not touching when stringing or laying out (see page 31).

Mixed fungus pie

Shortcrust pastry to line and top a pie dish
Filling: about 450g (1lb) mixed mushrooms and fungi e.g. ceps, chanterelles, honey fungi
fat for frying
1 onion finely chopped
parsley, chopped

seasoning
flour for thickening
chicken stock
lemon juice
white sauce flavoured with minced onion, lemon juice, paprika, mixed herbs, capers

Line a dish with pastry. Trim, clean and slice mushrooms and fungi. Sauté chopped onion gently in any cooking fat. Add chopped parsley and fungi and cook for a few minutes. Sprinkle them lightly with enough flour to absorb fat. Stir and add a squeeze of lemon juice and enough chicken stock to moisten the mixture. Fill mixture into lined pie dish. Make white sauce and use half in the pie, reserving the remainder to serve with it. Put the remaining crust on top of the filling, seal the edges and bake the pie in a hot oven 220°C (425°F, Gas 6) for ½ hour or until crust is golden-brown. A variation is to use, instead of pastry, alternate layers of cooked spaghetti and the mushroom filling in a pie dish. Top with breadcrumbs, dot with butter and bake till brown.

Honey fungus and onions

450g (1lb) honey fungus
350g (12oz) finely chopped onion
50g (2oz) butter
3 tablespoons oil

1 lemon
2 tablespoons finely chopped basil
2 tablespoons chopped parsley
seasoning

Heat together the oil and butter in a pan. Cook the onion until soft but not coloured. Clean the honey fungus and cut the stalks 1cm (½in) from the cap. Cut each fungus in two and plunge them into boiling water, to which a little lemon juice has been added, for 3 minutes. Drain and add to the onions. Cover and cook gently for a further 15 minutes.

Add seasoning and sprinkle with basil and parsley. Serve at once.

Jew's ear

Botanical name: *Auricularia auricula* or *Hirneola auricular-judae*
Family: *Auriculariaceae*

As its name suggests this tree fungus grows in the shape of an ear. It can be 3–10cm (1–4in) broad but with age it becomes more irregular in shape. Its upper surface is a reddish- or liver-brown colour, somewhat translucent and with a velvety grey bloom. When dry the fruit bodies of Jew's ear are hard and rigid, but become gelatinous and pliable again when moistened.

Jew's ear grows mostly on the bark of the common elder and occasionally on false acacia but seldom on other trees. It occurs almost all the year round but is more plentiful in October and November. Cut these fungi off with a knife, choosing young, pliable specimens.

USES
In spite of its unattractive appearance and thin flesh, Jew's ear is a good edible fungus. It should be well washed, finely sliced and stewed very gently in seasoned stock or milk for ½ to ¾ hour. If cooked for shorter time it may be tough and indigestible.

Salad of Jew's ear

225g (8oz) Jew's ear fungi	2 hard-boiled eggs
120g (4oz) ham	2 teaspoons chopped chervil
50g (2oz) cheese	mayonnaise
2 potatoes, cooked in their skins	

Wipe fungi and blanch them for 5 minutes in a pan of boiling salted water. Drain and leave to cool. Chop fungi, ham and cheese into small pieces and slice the potatoes and hard-boiled eggs. Put all into a salad bowl and mix well.

Carefully stir in sufficient mayonnaise to coat the pieces, sprinkle with chopped chervil and serve.

Morel

Botanical name: *Morchella esculenta* Family: *Ascomycetes*

Esculenta means good to eat and this is the biggest and best of the edible morels, a useful spring fungus. The morel has a hollow cap, more or less rounded or conical, grows to 5–12cm (2–5in) and varies in colour from pale yellowish-brown to blackish-grey. It is covered with sharp, sinuous ridges, irregularly arranged to form deep pits like a sponge or honeycomb. The base of the cap is attached to the paler, mealy stem, which is the same height as the cap.

Warning Although all varieties of morels are edible, a very poisonous fungus, *Gyromitra esculenta*, is similar enough to be mistaken for them. If there is any doubt in identification it is better to leave this type of fungus alone, especially if found in a coniferous wood.

Morels grow under leafy trees, in hedgerows, banks, damp meadows and where the ground is broken or has been burnt. They are fairly widespread in south-east England, but may appear locally in other areas. The best months to look for them are March, April and May.

USES

Collect only firm, dry, sweet-smelling specimens, discarding any that are faded, sodden or musty. Because of the morel's pitted surface and the occasional small fungi which may live on it, it is important to trim and wash morels thoroughly, changing the water several times. They should then be boiled in slightly salted water for a few minutes, drained, rinsed again under cold water and wiped firmly with a cloth or kitchen paper.

Morels provide a good aromatic flavouring, if only a few are added to soups, sauces, stuffings and in fillings for pies or vol au vents.

Use morels mixed with other fungi to make croquettes. After preparing the fungi as directed, stew them gently in good stock for a few minutes, then drain and chop them finely. Add ½ cup cream, 1 or 2 eggs, some grated onion, a good tablespoon of mixed fresh or dried herbs, salt, pepper and nutmeg, and finally enough breadcrumbs to make a firm mixture for shaping. Cover and refrigerate

146

for an hour before forming croquettes, frying them in shallow or deep fat.

Morels are excellent fungi for drying. Choose large specimens, clean well and cut in half. Dry by any of the methods described on pages 29–31. They may also be preserved in vinegar or in brine, or made into ketchup or sauce.

Egg-stuffed morels
Trim and wash morels as described. Cook them for a short time, about 3–5 minutes, in slightly salted boiling water. Rinse immediately in cold water and dry them on kitchen paper. Cut morels down the stalk and into the cap and fill the hollow with scrambled eggs flavoured with paprika, chopped chives or suitable wild herbs. Fry the morels in butter and serve on toast.

Morel filling for pancakes or tarts

600g (1½lb) morels	1 tablespoon parsley
275ml (10floz) well-flavoured stock	seasoning
1 heaped tablespoon flour	fat for frying

Trim, wash and boil morels as described above. Roughly chop morels and simmer gently in stock for 10 minutes. Heat fat in a pan, add parsley and flour. Cook for a minute or two, then add morels and stock. Stir to boiling point and as soon as it has thickened remove from heat and allow to cool.

Oyster mushroom

Botanical name: *Pleurotus ostreatus* Family: *Agaricaceae*

Beefsteak fungus

Botanical name: *Fistulina hepatica* Family: *Polyporaceae*

These bracket fungi grow on trees and not in the soil. The oyster mushroom has a shell-shaped cap with wavy edges 3–15cm (1–6in) across; it is moist and generally smooth, or may be slightly cracked. When young the colour of the cap is a greyish-blue, sometimes a deeper shade, almost black, turning brown with age. The broad, whitish gills extend down and join the stumpy stem, which is the same colour, its base covered in stiff little hairs. Oyster mushroom flesh is firm and off-white.

Beefsteak fungus looks rather like an ox tongue. It may be 5–30cm (2–12in) wide and has a sticky upper surface, reddish-brown in colour. The minute tubes are free from each other, they are a yellowish colour, flushed pink. There is little or no stem. The flesh of beefsteak fungus looks like red raw meat and when cut yields a reddish juice.

Oyster mushrooms are found growing in overhanging clusters on tree stumps, deciduous trees, especially beech, poplar and occasionally conifers, causing considerable damage. They start in autumn but in mild conditions continue through until spring. Beefsteak fungi are more common on living oak but attack other leafy trees as well. They are found from August to November.

USES

Oyster mushrooms have an interesting, fishy flavour and are delicious fried. Only young specimens should be collected and the caps used. Older ones tend to be tough and require lengthy cooking. But as they grow in such numbers it is easy to select soft young ones. Oyster mushrooms dry well, and slices fried in butter for a few minutes may also be frozen.

Although beefsteak fungus looks like meat it is a disappointing culinary species with a rather acrid taste. It requires the addition of strong-flavoured herbs, onions and garlic which should first be sautéed lightly in fat. Add the fungi, chopped small, and cook until tender.

Alternatively, beefsteak fungi may be simmered in a well-flavoured stock with vegetables, or added to a meat casserole.

Oyster mushrooms with red peppers

450g (1lb) oyster mushrooms	glass of white wine
2 red peppers	3 glasses stock
1 tomato	1 dessertspoon flour
2 onions, finely chopped	4 dessertspoons oil
2 cloves garlic, crushed	seasoning

Clean mushrooms and slice each in half. Cut up peppers and quarter the tomato. Heat oil in a pan add onion and garlic and soften but

148

do not colour. Add peppers, tomato and mushrooms and seasoning. Leave to cook for a further 10 minutes, stirring from time to time. Sprinkle in the flour and smooth with wine and stock. Cook over gentle heat for 20 minutes.

Serve hot with croutons of fried bread.

Oyster mushrooms in egg and breadcrumbs
Use only the young mushrooms, peeled and sliced. Cook slowly in a little water in a covered pan over low heat until tender. Drain the slices, sprinkle them with lemon juice, dip into seasoned flour, then in beaten egg and lastly in breadcrumbs. Sauté the slices in hot fat until golden.

Parasol mushroom

Botanical name: *Lepiota procera*
Lepiota rhacodes—Shaggy parasol
Family: *Agaricaceae*

The genus *Lepiota* contains some of the best-known esculents; the two described here are excellent for cooking and fairly common throughout Britain. Both are related to the *Amanita* fungi but parasols have no volva, which helps to distinguish them. The cap of the parasol mushroom starts egg-shaped and smooth, veiled by the skin which later forms the ring. The cap soon becomes conical or bell-shaped and eventually opens out like a parasol with a central protuberance. The diameter of an average specimen is 10–15cm (4–6in).

The surface of the expanded cap is dry, brown or grey brown and covered in dark-brown coarse scales, concentrically arranged, more numerous towards the centre. The stem, with its bulbous base, is belted with concentric brown stripes and is usually twice as long as the cap's diameter. The large double ring on the stem is white above and brown below, later becoming free so that it can be moved up and down. The white, crowded gills are separated from the stem by a distinct groove. The flesh of this big parasol is white and smooth with a pleasant, mealy smell, and does not change colour when cut.

Shaggy parasols are smaller versions of the large variety but are distinguished by their scale-free stems, scalier caps and thicker gills. In the button stage, shaggy parasols are brown and smooth, but as they open the thick, ragged, browny-grey scales form on the surface of the cap, except for the centre which remains smooth and brown without the prominent boss of the large parasol. The flesh of shaggy parasols is white but reddens when cut, most clearly seen in the stem.

From July to October parasol mushrooms can be found in large numbers growing in dry, sunny places near the edges of spruce forests and other woods, especially in clearings amongst grass and bracken. They also appear in orchards, gardens and hedgerows. Each plant develops alone, never in clusters and often in enormous circles. They can be seen from a distance because of their size and appearance.

Shaggy parasols prefer shady places. They grow from summer to autumn in dry woods, copses, often in clusters under pines, also in parks, gardens and on old compost heaps.

USES

The shaggy parasol and parasol mushroom are the only two parasols worth eating. All smaller varieties should be avoided. Be sure to check for the absence of a volva so that no poisonous *Amanita* are mistakenly collected.

Young parasols, when the cap is still closed, are best for cooking. They have a high protein content and a delicious flavour, like hazelnuts. Discard the stalks and use young caps which should only be scraped, not washed. Sauté or gently stew them in stock, do not overcook them or their delicate flavour and texture may be spoiled.

Parasols are also good seasoned, dipped in batter and deep fried until golden. Serve them with a herb- or garlic-flavoured mayonnaise.

Or stuff them with any savoury mix; or skewer with little strips of bacon on a toothpick and bake in the oven.

The large parasol is good for drying as it is slow to decay, transports well and may remain in good condition for several days. It may also be preserved by any of the suggested methods on pages 29–31.

Parasol fungi en casserole
Scrape caps and place them gills-up in a casserole pot. Season with

salt and paprika, sprinkle with lemon juice and put a dab of butter or margarine in the centre of each cap. Cover the pot and bake in a medium oven 180°C (350°F, Gas 4) for 20–40 minutes until tender.

Serve them as a vegetable or on toast, rice or mashed potatoes. Garnish with parsley, chives or other herbs.

Parasols in garlic butter

8 parasol fungi	8 dessertspoons chopped parsley
2 cloves of garlic, crushed	8 teaspoons breadcrumbs
120g (4oz) softened butter	

Carefully remove stalks of fungi and wipe the caps. Place caps, gills upwards, in a fireproof dish and leave covered in a low oven for 15 minutes.

Mix together softened butter, garlic, parsley and seasoning. Fill the fungus caps with garlic butter, sprinkle with breadcrumbs and put in a hot oven 200°C (400°F, Gas 6) for another 10 minutes.

Serve at once.

Puffballs

Botanical name: *Lycoperdon gigantum*—giant puffball
Lycoperdon perlatum or *gemnatum*—common puffball
Lycoperdon caelatum—mosaic puffball
Family: *Sclerodermataceae*

One of the most delectable edible fungi, the giant puffball is an extraordinary sight when you spot it in the grass, gleaming white like some mammoth egg. The size varies from a large turnip to more than 30cm (1ft) across. Young specimens are spherical; full-grown plants are more pumpkin-shaped, slightly flattened on top and grooved or folded at the bottom. The sterile base is very thin, often absent altogether, and rooted in the soil by a thick cord of mycelium which is the plant's 'spawn'. The wall in all puffballs is composed of two layers. The outer layer starts smooth and white like kid leather, later turning a greenish-yellow and breaking up, cracking and falling away from the inner layer: this is white at first, firm to the touch like cheese.

It is only when they are in this young, unripe condition that puff-balls are suitable as food. Do not eat them once the spores inside the ball have ripened into the yellowish-brown powdery mass which eventually disperses through a small hole at the top.

Of the other, smaller varieties of edible puffball, probably a dozen or more, two are worth collecting. The mosaic puffball is 6–10cm (2–4in) wide, cup-shaped, and open at the top. Whitish-grey in colour when young, it soon cracks and peels, turning a cinnamon-brown shade.

The common puffball, only 2–5cm (1–2in) wide and up to 8cm (3in) high has more of a stem and is recognised by the large, prominent, conical thorns on the white, pear-shaped head. These thorns are easily rubbed off the surface, leaving a pattern of square hollows. Like other puffballs, the flesh soon discolours and breaks down into a greenish-yellow powder.

Always pick and eat the common puffball while still white and young: in fact, a good rule is to pick only white and creamy specimens to avoid collecting the slightly poisonous common earthball (*Scleroderma aurantium* or *citrinum*). This is brown and scaly, the skin cracking with age. It gives off an intense, spicy smell and is found in pine and birch woods on peaty subsoil.

The giant puffball with its short lifespan of only a few days, grows in open fields, under hedges and near compost heaps. It appears first in about August and continues through to October. The mosaic puffball is found in similar places but on more sandy soil in August and September. The small common variety grows in woods, also in August and September.

USES

The flesh of young giant puffballs is pure creamy-white, solid but spongy. It is like sweetbreads in texture and flavour. To make sure it is fit to eat, cut off the base of the puffball and check that it has not started to ripen and discolour. Peel the outer skin only if leathery. Cut the flesh with a bread knife in ½ inch slices or rounds. Fry the slices in butter and serve with a squeeze of lemon juice. For a better flavour, egg and breadcrumb the slices first; dip the slices in beaten egg with a little milk and use fine breadcrumbs for coating. Allow these to stand awhile before frying.

Whole fried puffballs
Choose small firm young puffballs, about the size of hazel nuts. In a pan heat together equal quantities of butter and oil—sufficient to cover the puffballs. When really hot drop in the puffballs and turn them all the time whilst cooking. Cook them until golden-yellow. Drain and serve at once sprinkled with salt.

The very small puffballs may be sliced and eaten raw in salads.

Puffballs cannot be preserved and must only be eaten fresh.

Puffballs with barberries

12 puffballs, hen's egg size	bay leaf
seasoned flour	sauce: butter, cornflour
milk to cover	garnish: barberries, parsley
½ onion, sliced	

Wipe puffballs carefully, check that they are firm and white. Roll in seasoned flour and put them in a deep, heavy saucepan. Pour over enough milk just to cover them, add bayleaf and sliced onion. Simmer gently till soft. Lift puffballs out carefully on to a hot dish and keep warm. Make a white sauce with butter, cornflour and the milk in which the puffballs were simmered; pour it over the puffballs.

Garnish with sprigs of fresh, softened, scarlet barberries and chopped parsley for a really attractive dish.

Saffron milk cap

Botanical name: *Lactarius deliciosus* Family: *Russulineae*

The saffron milk cap is easily distinguished from other less pleasant *Lactarius* fungi by the saffron-coloured cap and stem, as well as the milky juice it exudes when cut or broken. Most other milk caps have white 'milk'. The cap of saffron milk cap is 3–10cm (1–4in) wide, convex when young with its margin unrolled. Later it develops a central depression and may even be funnel-shaped. The colour is orange brick with concentric zones of darker markings. With age, or when handled, the cap stains green as do the narrow, crowded gills. The stem, 2–5cm (1–2in) tall, is a slightly paler orange and spotted green when bruised. It soon becomes hollow. The whitish

153

flesh turns orange immediately when broken, then green.

All parts of this fungus, especially the gills, exude drops of a bright saffron-coloured 'milk' which turns green on exposure to air.

The saffron milk cap is found from August to November, mainly in grass under young conifers, also in damp meadows surrounded by woods and in woodland glades. Only sound specimens should be collected, and to identify correctly be sure the 'milk' is carrot-coloured.

USES

Saffron milk caps have a pleasant, spicy flavour and aroma. They are best fried and should not be stewed or an unpleasant taste may develop. Always wash milk caps before cooking. Trim stems, leaving about an inch.

To fry them, heat a little oil or butter in pan, put in prepared milk caps, stalks up, and fill the hollow stem with olive or other good oil. Fry till golden-brown. Serve with lemon wedges.

Milk caps may also be stuffed or coated in egg and breadcrumbs or batter before frying. Very young specimens are suitable for eating raw in salads or as an hors d'oeuvre. Wash and trim milk caps, then marinate them in a dressing of oil and lemon juice. They may also be blanched before marinating. Milk caps cannot be dried but may be preserved by pickling in vinegar (p35).

Saffron milk cap soup

450g (1lb) young fresh saffron milk caps
1 medium onion, chopped small
2 small cloves garlic, crushed
2 small potatoes, chopped

1¼ litres (2pt) stock
120g (4oz) lean minced pork
75g (3oz) grated cheese
olive oil
seasoning

Clean milk caps thoroughly and mince coarsely. Into a pan put 2 dessertspoons oil and minced milk caps. Cook over gentle heat until the milk caps are almost dry. In another pan, cook chopped onion and garlic till soft and golden brown and add to milk caps. Add potatoes, pork and stock. Season to taste. Simmer gently 45–60 minutes, adjust seasoning if necessary.

Serve very hot with grated cheese sprinkled on top.

St George's mushroom

Botanical name: *Tricholoma gambosum* Family: *Agaricaceae*

The name of this excellent mushroom refers to St George's Day in April when it is often to be seen growing in fairy rings in the grass. Related to the blewits, St George's mushroom is a pale creamy-white or buff colour, with a soft skin like kid leather. The fleshy cap, 5–15cm (2–6in) across, is rounded, hemispherical to convex, rather irregularly shaped with a turned-in margin, sometimes cracked lengthwise. The arched gills are narrow, crowded and attached to the short thick stem, which is often swollen at the base. The flesh of St George's mushroom is white and thick, especially in the middle, and has a strong mealy or floury smell.

Warning: St George's mushrooms should not be collected by beginners because they have white gills and resemble the red-staining Inocybe *(Inocybe patouillardii)*, a dangerously poisonous fungus, which also appears in April and May and looks white and appetising when young. Later on it turns a pinky-yellow colour and finally brownish-red. When cut, it does not change colour immediately but slowly becomes red, when there is less danger of mistaking it for St George's mushroom. Another dangerous double in structure and habitat is the livid Entoloma *(Entoloma lividum* or *sinuatum)*. Here, the difference to look for is the pink gills in the mature specimens. But again, when young, the gills are white like those of St George's mushroom. The seasons are different. Livid *Entoloma* grows in summer and autumn in woods and under beech, oak and hornbeam trees.

St George's mushroom, like the morel, is one of the few early spring mushrooms to be found in thick, grassy places, in chalky fields, on open downs and slopes, at edges of woods and in orchards. It grows on until midsummer, often in small or large rings. Red-staining inocybe grows on chalky soil in beech and other deciduous woods.

USES

St George's mushroom tastes and smells strongly of new meal. Remove the stalks, slice the large caps and leave small ones whole. Wipe off any dirt or grit, but do not wash the mushrooms.

Young dry specimens are excellent fried or grilled, but they toughen with long cooking. Add them to sauces or stews for the last few minutes of cooking.

To fry them, melt butter or oil in pan, add a few sliced onions and soften them before adding the mushrooms. Turn frequently while cooking until the juices flow. To absorb the liquid, sprinkle a little flour into the pan, stir and add some fresh or sour cream, season and cook a few minutes longer. In place of cream, use stock and lemon juice or white wine. Sprinkle chopped parsley, chives or herbs of your choice and serve the mushrooms on toast or rice.

Use St George's mushrooms in place of cultivated mushrooms in omelettes and pancakes, kebabs, stuffed or in stuffings, in soufflés and as a vegetable on their own. Mix with other vegetables such as courgettes or broccoli.

St George's mushrooms may be dried but need to be cut into slices beforehand.

Other methods for preserving are described in Chapter 2.

Mushroom soup

450g (1lb) St George's mushrooms	150ml (¼pt) cream or milk or
1 onion, chopped	white wine
½ cup tender celery, chopped	salt and pepper
2 tablespoons flour	pinch mace or nutmeg
1.1l (2pt) chicken or white stock	milled parsley
1 egg yolk	

Trim, clean and slice mushrooms, discarding woody stems. Heat fat in heavy pan, add chopped onions and celery and cook over gentle heat for 5 minutes. Add mushroom slices, cook for a few minutes, then pour in half the stock. Simmer until vegetables are tender.

Liquidize vegetables in electric blender or pass through a sieve or vegetable mill. Return purée to saucepan. Make a smooth paste of the flour with a little stock. Beat in egg yolk and some of the hot soup, then return to pan. Gradually add remaining stock and cream or wine. Season, reheat stirring all the time until thick and smooth, but do not allow to boil.

Correct seasoning and serve soup liberally sprinkled with chopped parsley.

St George's bread

450g (1lb) St George's mushrooms
1 stick French bread
1 clove garlic
150g (5oz) butter

5 teaspoons parsley
75g (3oz) cream
lemon juice
seasoning

Finely chop garlic and parsley and mix with 100g (3½oz) softened butter. Slice the loaf lengthwise but not right through, and remove the crumb. Spread with parsley butter. Wrap in foil and put into a hot oven 200°C (400°F, Gas 6), for 10 minutes. Meanwhile sauté cleaned, chopped St George's mushrooms, using caps only, in 50g (2oz) butter. Add a little lemon juice, seasoning and then the cream; mix well. Fill the bread cavity with the mixture, rewrap the loaf in foil and heat in the oven for a further 5 minutes.

Serve with salad.

8

NUTS

Nuts provide concentrated food, rich in protein, vitamins and minerals, with a high calorie value due to the absence of water and large amounts of fat. With the exception of chestnuts, they are an alkali-forming food, unlike meat which is acid-forming.

From late summer on, hazelnuts, sweet chestnuts, beech nuts, and occasionally almonds and walnuts, may be found growing in hedgerows, scrubland, woods and parks throughout Britain; but remember that small animals and birds also depend on these wild foods for their winter survival.

Ripe acorn kernels may be ground, roasted twice and used as a coffee substitute; otherwise the prolific crop from our oak trees is not much use as human food, but can provide animal fodder.

Almond

Botanical names: *Prunus amygdalus var. dulcis*—sweet almond
Prunus amygdalus var. amara—bitter almond
Family: *Rosaceae*

A member of the plum, cherry and peach family, the almond tree grows to a height of 9m (30ft). In March its lovely pink blossoms on leafless branches are a familiar sight, for it is often grown for decorative purposes. The variety which bears the sweet almond has widely spreading branches and lance-shaped, serrated leaves with short stalks. After the blossom has fallen the nut develops. It is covered with a hard, downy, outer coat, a dull red colour, tinged green. When ripe it splits open and the buff-coloured, pitted shell

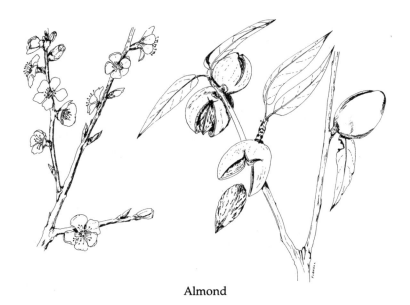

Almond

containing the almond kernel drops out. The almond itself is round at one end, pointed at the other and covered with a brown skin.

The bitter almond, only used commercially for producing almond essence, is not otherwise edible. It contains prussic acid, used in certain medicines. The trees are similar to the sweet almond but have large white flowers which gradually turn pink at the base of the petal. The nut is shorter, broader, and less regular than the sweet variety.

Sweet almonds are extremely nutritious and contain protein, carbohydrates, vitamins A and B, and various minerals. Their high percentage of fat yields a fine, odourless oil with a good nutty flavour. Sweet almond trees are not indigenous to Britain but have naturalised here since their introduction by the Romans. Today they flourish in town and country gardens, in open or sheltered positions on most soils. Some trees may be found growing wild as escapes from old orchards or nutteries. In a good season the nuts ripen from late August, but often not at all after a cold wet summer.

USES

Sweet almonds can be used in the same way as hazelnuts in nearly

159

all the recipes. To make almond cream, select about thirty perfect sweet almonds and remove their skins by blanching. Leave them to soak in cold water for 2–3 hours. Take out, dry in a clean cloth and pound the nuts to a pulp in pestle and mortar, or put them in an electric liquidizer with 50ml (2fl oz) water, turn to lowest speed for a few seconds, then turn up to full speed for 4–6 minutes. The mixture should be smooth and like thick cream. Use this nut cream to replace heavy cream in a recipe, or dilute it with warm water or fruit juice with a little sweetening for a nutritious drink.

Nut milk or fruit nut milk, often more easily digested than cow's milk, may be used for children or in special diets where cow's milk is not tolerated.

Almond plum tart

shortcrust pastry
½kg (1lb) plums
50g (2oz) ground almonds
50g (2oz) sugar

3 tablespoons breadcrumbs
½ teaspoon ground cinnamon
a little butter or margarine

Wipe and halve plums, removing stones. Line a 20cm (8in) flan case with pastry and sprinkle the ground almonds over the bottom to form a thick layer. Place the plums on top and add a little sugar. Mix together the breadcrumbs, cinnamon and remaining sugar and spread over plums. Dot with butter or margarine. Bake in a fairly hot oven 200°C (400°F, Gas 6) for 30–40 minutes.

Rosehip macaroons

3 tablespoons rosehip purée (page 62).
3 tablespoons castor sugar
225g (8oz) icing sugar

2 whites of egg
225g (8oz) ground blanched almonds
halved blanched almonds

Stir the castor sugar into rosehip purée, made from fresh or dried hips, and boil together for a few minutes. Allow to cool. Beat egg whites and icing sugar until frothy. Stir in rosehip purée and ground almonds until mixture is firm.

On a well-oiled tin (or rice paper if available) place small heaps of the mixture, then flatten them slightly and put a halved blanched almond in the centre of each.

Bake at 150°C (300°F, Gas 2) for about 25 minutes until golden and crisp.

Cream cheese salad with almonds

150g (6oz) cream cheese
2 tablespoons finely chopped
  blanched almonds
1 tablespoon caraway seeds

single cream
corn salad leaves
2 cooked beetroots
1 tablespoon chopped chives

Cream together the cheese, almonds, caraway and single cream. Wash and dry corn salad leaves and arrange on a flat dish. Peel beetroots and cut into thin strips. Arrange them in squares on the corn salad and heap cheese mixture inside each square. Decorate with chopped chives.

Beech

Botanical name: *Fagus sylvatica* Family: *Fagaceae*

One of our most beautiful trees with its smooth, grey bark, the beech tree can reach a great age and height. Native in the south, beeches are found in large woods, mainly on chalk or sandy soils. Further north, this is a planted species. In April or May the pale green, almost transparent leaves and yellow catkin flowers appear together on the same twig; but beech trees do not flower freely every year and only produce their fruits, the beech nuts or beech-mast, every third or fourth year. Really good mast years occur every five to ten years in England. The nuts, green at first, ripen in pairs inside a prickly brown cup. By September or October, the husk opens into four lobes and releases the ripe, brown, three-sided nuts, the favourite food of a number of woodland animals and birds. Beech nuts contain a valuable vegetable oil as well as protein. Gather them in late autumn as soon as they fall.

USES
Beech nuts are mostly valued for the excellent oil they yield, used in the past to light oil lamps as well as for cooking. The nut kernels may be eaten raw or baked until crisp and sprinkled with salt as appetisers.

Beech—flowers and nuts

A flour or meal for use in baking can be made from dried and finely ground nuts. This has a pleasant, nutty flavour and can replace some of the flour in cake and biscuit recipes, as in the recipe given for beech nut crescents.

Young beech leaves are also edible. Pick them in spring when they are a translucent pale green, cook and purée them like spinach.

To express oil from beechmast may be difficult without an oil press. The nuts should be thoroughly cleaned and ground up in their shells. An electric mincing attachment to a strong mixing machine may be suitable. Place the minced nuts in a clean muslin bag and put under weights if an oil press is not available. A pound (450g) of nuts yields about 75ml (3floz) of oil, one of the best salad and cooking oils with a pleasant, mild flavour. The oil keeps a long time without going rancid, longer than most vegetable oils. Pour the freshly pressed oil into clean crocks or bottles, cork down and store the containers in a cool, dark place. The pulp remaining after the pressing makes a nutritious addition to cattle cake and animal fodders.

Beech nuts may be stored in their shells, or store the kernels whole or chopped in containers in the fridge or freezer, as for other nuts.

Beech nut crescents

225g (8oz) butter   250g (9oz) flour
50g (2oz) sugar   120g (4oz) beech nuts
vanilla essence

Cream the butter, vanilla essence and sugar until soft and fluffy. Gradually add the flour and nuts minced finely. Knead the paste until smooth. With floured hands shape pieces into small crescents, and bake on greased tins in a fairly hot oven 180–200°C (350–400°F, Gas 4–6) for 10 to 15 minutes or until golden brown. Roll crescents in sugar while hot.

Salted beech nuts

Shell beech nuts and roast them on a flat tin in a hot oven for 5–10 minutes. Turn off oven. Take out and peel the nuts, then replace them in the cooling oven to dry.

When crisp, sprinkle them with salt and serve as appetisers, or as a substitute for other salted nuts.

Chestnut (sweet chestnut, spanish chestnut)

Botanical name: *Castanea sativa* Family: *Fagaceae*

The sweet chestnut is not related to the horse chestnut—*Aesculus hippocastanum* (the 'conker' tree) and *Aesculus carnea* (the red-flowering horse chestnut). Horse chestnuts are not to be eaten, although with other parts of the tree they are used commercially in a variety of ways.

Sweet (or Spanish) chestnuts, like the beech and the oak of the same family, are tall, majestic trees growing to a height of 30m (90ft). The smooth bark is fissured with deep, spiralling ridges up and down the trunk. Slender, pointed leaves, 20–25cm (8–10in) long, are saw-toothed and deeply veined, glossy green in spring turning in autumn to rich golden shades. The long thin spikes of male and female catkin flowers appear long after the leaves are fully grown, as late as July or August, a distinguishing characteristic of the sweet chestnut. The nuts, two to five together, develop inside a prickly green ball or husk, which splits open in October to release the shiny brown chestnuts. These are flat on one side with a large pale scar where they were fastened to the husk.

163

Sweet chestnut—flowers and nuts

Horse chestnuts look quite different, though they are also very tall, handsome trees. Their palmate leaves develop from big sticky buds. Lovely spikes of white or deep-pink, candle-like flowers, according to the variety, are a familiar sight in spring. The inedible single nuts or 'conkers' are contained in green husks studded with short spines.

Sweet chestnuts contain more carbohydrates and less fat and minerals than other nuts, but are equally rich in vitamins C and B1. Sweet chestnut trees were probably introduced to this country by the Romans. They were extensively planted and are found today in parks, woods and large forests; they are also often coppiced for their useful timber. Chestnuts grow best on dry sandy soil but are well distributed throughout Britain.

The nuts are ready for collecting in autumn as soon as they split open and start falling.

164

Chestnuts have to be shelled and peeled before eating or cooking. Before shelling, put the nuts into a bowl of cold water and discard any that float, for these will be mouldy. Next, follow one or other of the methods for shelling and peeling described in Chapter 2.

Chestnuts are traditionally roasted in hot embers or an oven, peeled and eaten hot. They may be boiled and served with vegetables such as Brussels sprouts, onions and cabbage.

Puréed, they can replace mashed potatoes. Cook the nuts until tender in vegetable stock or milk flavoured with a piece of whole cinnamon and celeriac root or celery leaves. Rub the nuts through a sieve, or purée by other means available. Season well with salt, pepper and a pinch of sugar. This purée can be served in a number of ways; as a vegetable on its own, in a bechamel sauce sprinkled with grated cheese and browned in a hot oven, in stuffings, or as a soup cooked with potatoes and carrots.

Delicious hot and cold chestnut sweets and puddings can also be made. Try chestnut mount crème: after boiling the nuts in milk sweetened with vanilla flavoured sugar, mince or grate them into a mound on a serving plate. Cover the mound with sweetened whipped cream. Alternatively, mince the chestnuts onto fresh, bottled or tinned fruit and decorate with whipped cream as before.

Meringues may be filled with this chestnut 'vermicelli' and topped with whipped cream. For a good, hot pudding make the sweetened chestnut purée, add to it a tablespoon of butter creamed with 4 egg yolks and 120g (4oz) or less of sugar. Fold in egg whites beaten to a froth and bake in a greased dish in a medium oven 180°C (350°F, Gas 4) for approximately 50 minutes.

Chestnuts are excellent in cakes, biscuits and pastries. They may be preserved in sugar or syrup, or dipped in whisked egg white, rolled in sugar and dried in a low oven.

Chestnut biscuits

675g (1½lb) chestnuts	1 large egg
120g (4oz) butter or margarine	vanilla essence
120g (4oz) flour	½ teaspoon baking powder
75g (3oz) sugar	

Make a slit in each chestnut with a sharp knife and bake them in the oven until soft. Take off the skins and grind the nuts up coarsely. Put the flour and baking powder into a bowl and rub in the butter. Add the sugar and chestnuts. Bind the mixture with the beaten egg flavoured with vanilla essence. Roll the pastry out on a floured board and cut into small rounds. Lay these on a greased baking tin, prick each with a fork and bake in a medium oven 180°C (350°F, Gas 4) for about 20 minutes.

Candied chestnuts

peeled chestnuts
450g (1lb) sugar

275ml (10floz) water
150ml (5floz) rum (optional)

Cook peeled chestnuts in gently boiling water until tender but still whole. Drain and leave to cool. Heat sugar and water stirring until sugar is dissolved, add the rum. Bring to the boil and boil to the thread stage, 105°C (220°F). Skim to keep syrup clear. Remove from heat. Dip each chestnut into the syrup making sure it is completely coated. Stand them on a wire cake tray to drain and dry.

French chestnut soup

225g (8oz) peeled chestnuts
1–2 large potatoes
2 large carrots

salt, paprika
850ml (1½pt) vegetable stock
croutons of fried bread

Peel chestnuts by the method described on page 26. Put them in a large saucepan with the carrots cut in half and potatoes quartered. Add salt, paprika and 575ml (1pt) of the stock. Simmer until chestnuts are tender, then purée the nuts and vegetables in a vegetable mill or electric blender, or by passing through a sieve.

Replace purée in saucepan and dilute with rest of stock. Adjust seasoning if needed and heat up.

Serve soup with fried croutons.

Chestnut stuffing

450g (1lb) peeled chestnuts
vegetable stock
50g (2oz) melted butter or margarine

120g (4oz) dry breadcrumbs
38ml (1½floz) single cream
1 teaspoon salt
ground ginger, nutmeg, paprika

Simmer peeled chestnuts in stock to cover until tender. Purée them by rubbing through a sieve, or in a vegetable mill or liquidizer. Mix in melted butter or margarine, breadcrumbs and cream. Season with salt, ginger, nutmeg and paprika to taste.

This stuffing may be used in all poultry and game and for filling suitable vegetables such as marrows, cucumbers, tomatoes and peppers. See stuffed tomatoes using hazel-nuts, page 172.

Cabbage and chestnuts

1 medium firm red or white cabbage	450g (1lb) cooking apples
37g (1½oz) cooking fat or 2 table-spoons oil	1 teaspoon sugar
	good pinch ground cloves
2 chopped onions	2–3 tablespoons lemon juice
seasoning	2 tablespoons single cream
150g (5oz) peeled cooked chestnuts	275ml (½pt) vegetable stock

Peel chestnuts by simmering gently in water until tender. Slice finely or grate the cabbage, then wash and drain it. Fry chopped onions in heated cooking fat or oil until golden but still soft. Add cabbage and seasoning, continue to cook a few minutes. Turn heat right down, cover pan with lid and allow to simmer gently for about 10 minutes. Add chestnuts and apples peeled and thinly sliced. Season with sugar and ground cloves. Add stock and continue to cook over low heat until tender and liquid is absorbed.

Finally stir in lemon juice and cream, and serve at once.

Hazel (hazel-nut, cob-nut, filbert, hale, hasketts, woodnut)

Botanical name: *Corylus avellana* Family: *Corylaceae*

Hazel is a native shrub, usually a thick bush in hedgerows or gardens. It has smooth, peeling bark and often produces root suckers. Hazel twigs are used for divining rods. If left to grow as a tree, hazel can reach a height of 6m (20ft).

In January the familiar, long, brown, male catkins appear. These lambs tails grow from inconspicuous, green stamen catkins formed the previous summer, their yellow pollen soon fertilising the female catkins which form the nuts. The toothed, oval leaves of hazel are conspicuously veined and downy on both sides. They start a clear green but turn dull red and finally yellow.

Hazel-nuts are pale green to start and ripen to a glossy brown; the scaly leaves which covered the bud grow and thicken to form the covering or husk. There are two varieties of hazel-nuts, the cob and filbert. The cob is oval-shaped and only partly covered by the husk; filberts are oblong and entirely encased in a long, tapering husk. The most common variety grown in England is the Kentish cob, which is really a filbert.

Hazel-nuts are rich in vegetable protein, a fatty oil, carbohydrate, vitamins and minerals. They are most nutritious eaten raw soon after gathering.

Hazel-nut bushes and trees are widespread throughout Britain, common in hedgerows, woods, near quarries and along river banks. The nuts are ready for gathering from late September to October when they fall easily from the husk. Those out of reach can be gently shaken out of the tree, although many will already be on the ground among the similar-coloured fallen leaves, where squirrels, mice and birds may find them first.

USES

Use hazel-nuts whole, chopped or milled in sandwiches, raw or cooked salads, hot and cold desserts, in cakes, breads and confectionery. Sprinkle milled hazel-nuts on to breakfast muesli with other wild fruits or berries. Add the ground nut-meats to breadcrumbs for extra nutrition in au gratin dishes, or use them for meatless recipes such as the vegetarian roast, page 170.

For a substantial three-decker sandwich filling, mix together chopped hard-boiled eggs, grated cheese, milled hazel-nuts and seasoning. Cream a tablespoon of butter, add the egg and nut mixture with 3 tablespoons lemon juice and one small raw egg. Chill the mixture before spreading on wholemeal bread; cover each slice with wild salad greens.

Include nut-meats in fruit salads, in filling for baked apples and in ice creams. Make the ice cream as the recipe below and top it with this hazel-nut brittle: melt in a heavy pan over low heat 1 cup of sugar, stirring constantly. When syrup is light brown stir in and coat well 1 cup toasted hazel-nuts. Pour the mixture onto a buttered plate or tin, allow to cool then crack into pieces.

Use hazel-nuts in fruit and nut cakes, in breads and to flavour cake fillings. Delicious nut brioches may be made with a yeast dough rolled out and cut into 15cm (6in) triangles. Make a filling with 50g (2oz) each of butter and sugar creamed together with an egg. Mix in the grated peel of a lemon, a tablespoon lemon juice, a tablespoon flour and 50g (2oz) milled hazel-nuts. Spread some filling on each triangle of dough, roll up from one corner and form into crescents. Place on greased tin and leave in warm place to rise for ¾ hour. Brush the crescents with egg and bake in a hot oven, 200°C (400°F, Gas 6) for 40 minutes. The brioches may be iced after baking.

For a good cold dessert, add 75–120g (3–4oz) roasted, skinned and ground hazel-nuts to a custard cream made with 575ml (1pt) milk sweetened with 50g (2oz) vanilla-flavoured sugar, 2 eggs and a dessertspoon cornflour. Add the ground nuts with the sugar and vanilla to the boiling milk. In a bowl, blend the cornflour with a little cold milk, mix in the beaten eggs and gradually add the boiling milk. Pour back into the pan, bring to boil again, whisking continuously. Pour into a clean bowl and when quite cold fold in 150ml (¼pt) whipped cream. Serve sprinkled with ground hazel-nuts.

Use hazel-nuts to make candies and sweets. For hazel-nut balls: mix ground hazel-nuts with a little condensed milk, softened margarine or butter, some sweet chocolate powder or cocoa and icing sugar. Form into balls and roll them in chocolate powder or cocoa. For chocolate rolls: cream together 50–75g (2–3oz) sugar and 2 egg yolks. Melt in a bowl over hot water 50g (2oz) dark chocolate, add 18g (¾oz) butter or margarine and when melted whisk in creamed eggs and sugar. Add 50g (2oz) chopped nuts and 25g (1oz) raisins. Mix well, cool and put mixture onto a well-sugared board. When cold, form into narrow rolls and coat in sugar.

Leave to dry, then cut the rolls into thin slices.

Hazel-nuts store well in the shell. They should be dry and hard. Collect the nuts if possible during a dry spell. Spread them out on sacking or other flat surface for a day or two, turning them over occasionally. Remove husks and discard any discoloured nuts. Store the sound ones in:

1 Boxes between layers of bran, sand or sawdust with a good covering layer on top. Keep in a warm dry place away from frost and pests.

2 In jars or tins, tightly packed and covered with a layer of salt before fitting lid. Store as above, or bury containers two to three feet

deep in the ground for protection.

3 In the fridge in airtight containers, either in shells or the kernels milled or chopped.

4 In the freezer, as for fridge and wrapped in the usual way for frozen food.

Vegetarian nut roast

2 cups dried pulses (peas, beans, lentils), soaked for 12 hours; or: 2 cups oatflakes soaked for 2 hours	parsley cooking fat 1 cup milled hazel-nuts
2 cups soft brown bread	2 eggs, separated
1 onion, 1 leek, 2–3 ribs celery, finely chopped	mixed herbs and seasoning breadcrumbs

Cook pulses in the water in which they were soaked for 2–3 hours until tender (or 10–20 minutes in pressure cooker according to maker's directions). If using oatflakes, cook them in their water for 10 minutes. Cover bread with boiling water, stir till smooth. Fry chopped vegetables and parsley in hot fat for 5–10 minutes, then add bread mix and continue frying until water is absorbed. Allow to cool, mix in nuts, cooked pulses or oatflakes, yolks of eggs, plenty of mixed wild or cultivated herbs and seasoning.

Form a loaf, roll it in egg white and then in breadcrumbs, repeat several times. Put loaf into baking tin with hot fat and bake in a fairly hot oven 200°C (400°F, Gas 6) for ¾ hour, basting frequently.

Wild vegetables au gratin

Choose wild hop shoots, samphire, seakale, burdock or young elder shoots. Prepare and cook shoots in boiling salted water. Do not overcook. Drain well, arrange the shoots in a baking dish and pour over them a bechamel sauce flavoured with a wild bouquet garni and season with salt, pepper and nutmeg. Spread on top a mixture consisting of 1 egg and a little milk beaten together, added to ½ cup each of breadcrumbs and grated cheese and 5 tablespoons milled hazel-nuts. Season with salt and paprika. Brown in a hot oven for about 20 minutes.

Wild fruit and nut pudding

1 Grate 225g (½lb) stale brown bread into a bowl, mix in 75g (3oz) sugar, the grated rind of a lemon and 25–50g (1–2oz) milled hazel-

nuts. Using 450g (1lb) of fresh or preserved soft fruits, fill a serving bowl with alternate layers of bread mix and fruit.
Top with whipped cream and chill.
2 Cream together 50g (2oz) butter, 2 egg yolks, 3–4 tablespoons sugar. Soak 75–120g (3–4oz) brown bread soaked in milk, add 75g (3oz) milled hazel or other nuts. Add prepared and mashed bilberries or other wild berries in season. Fold in stiffly beaten egg white. Bake in buttered fireproof dish for 30–40 minutes in medium oven 180°C (350°F, Gas 4). Or steam the mixture in greased covered pudding basin for 1 hour.

Hazel-nut ice cream

120g (4oz) milled hazel-nuts	1 teaspoon butter
575ml (1pt) milk	75g (3oz) sugar
yolks of 4 eggs	

Simmer the milk and nuts in a pan for 20 minutes. Put butter, sugar and egg yolks into a double saucepan and beat together. Gradually add the milk and nuts to this mixture, beating until it becomes thick. Strain into a container and when cool put into the freezer. Freeze for an hour until just firm. Remove and beat again before returning it to freezer. This produces a really smooth ice cream.

Uncooked nut cake

200g (7oz) oatflakes	½ cup milled or finely chopped hazel-nuts
2–3 bananas or 2 grated carrots	
1 tablespoon lemon juice	fresh fruit
1 tablespoon brown sugar	whipped cream or nut cream (p160) for topping
cream to mix	
2 tablespoons golden syrup	

Mix together all ingredients except fruit and topping. Work into a thick paste with a little cream. Spread and press down mixture on a large plate or flat dish or tin lined with foil. Cover mixture with fresh, sweetened, juicy fruit and top with whipped cream. If using nut cream flavour it with apple juice, a few drops of lemon juice and honey or sugar to taste.

Hazel-nut brandy snaps
Cream together 2 eggs and 120g (4oz) sugar until fluffy. Add 120g

171

(4oz) flour, a pinch of salt, 2 tablespoons milled hazel-nuts and 4 tablespoons water. Work to a smooth paste. Roll out thinly and cut into small squares. Bake on a well-oiled tin in a slow oven 150°C (300°F, Gas 2) until a golden-brown colour. Take out and roll up each square quickly over the handle of a large wooden spoon.

Fill the rolls with whipped cream or the nut cream, as in the previous recipe.

Wild fruit jam with hazel-nuts
Take 450g (1lb) each of wild blackberries, crab apples, elderberries, and 225g (½lb) each rowan berries, hips and haws and 120g (¼lb) of hazel-nuts. First simmer hips, haws, elderberries, rowan berries and crab apples in about a teacup of water until tender. Press the cooked fruit through a sieve and put the pulp in a pan with washed blackberries and finely ground hazel-nuts. Simmer for 15 minutes. Add an equal weight of sugar, bring back to the boil and boil for about 20 minutes or until a little sets when tested on a cold plate.

Pot and tie down while still hot.

Hazel-nut-stuffed tomatoes

4–6 large ripe tomatoes	pinch salt, paprika
1 cup (about 225g) drained pine-apple cubes	2 tablespoons mayonnaise
	whole hazel-nuts for garnish
50g (2oz) coarsely chopped hazel-nuts	lettuce leaves

Scald and skin tomatoes. Cut off tops and scoop out tomato pulp, taking care to leave a large opening. Purée the pulp with the drained pineapple cubes and mix the purée with chopped nuts, salt, paprika and mayonnaise.

Fill tomato cases with the mixture and serve on lettuce or other salad leaves.

Walnut

Botanical name: *Juglans regia* Family: *Juglandaceae*

The walnut tree is a tall, handsome tree with a large spreading top. The smooth, grey trunk becomes rugged with age and reaches a great thickness. It takes about twenty-five years for a walnut tree to come into full fruit.

The large, pinnate leaves begin a dull red colour but when fully grown are a clear, deep green and extremely fragrant when crushed. Solitary male catkins and female flowers grow on the same tree. From mid-April to May the flowers, which take a year to develop, bloom before the tree is in full leaf. The nut develops from the tiny seed-flower growing at the end of the twig. By July they are plum-sized with a soft, green husk, and ready for collecting if the unripe walnut is wanted. When fully ripe the husk turns brown and splits open to release the walnut.

Green walnuts have a very high content of vitamin C, higher than rosehips. They also contain vitamin B, protein, carbohydrate, tannins, oils and minerals. Unlike other nuts they are an acid-forming food and unsuitable for babies.

Walnut trees are not truly wild or native to this country, but they were once widely planted along roadsides, in avenues, walks and orchards on large estates. Although so many trees have been felled for their valuable timber, some walnut trees may still be found in old woods, parks and large gardens. Collect the ripe walnuts in late

Walnut—flowers and nuts

173

September and October as soon as they fall, or have been shaken down, from the tree.

Unripe green walnuts can be added to enrich other fruit jams with vitamin C, or made into a nutritious marmalade. They may also be pickled or made into ketchups.

Walnut oil expressed from the kernels makes a good salad and cooking oil and is used for nut butter.

Ripe walnuts add protein, substance and flavour to salads. Add them chopped or whole to mixed green salads, apple and celery salad, to cream cheese, in stuffed tomatoes and with mayonnaise in sandwich spreads. Use chopped or milled walnuts in fresh fruit salads and other uncooked desserts, cooked cold sweets, steamed puddings and in breads, cakes, biscuits, pastries and sweetmeats.

To store walnuts treat them like hazel-nuts (pp169–70) and when the husks have fallen off, clean off traces of fibre from the shells before storing. Walnuts may also be stored in the fridge or freezer in their shells, or shelled and put whole or chopped into containers.

Green walnut marmalade
To every 225g (½lb) green walnuts allow 575ml (1pt) boiling water, 350g (¾lb) sugar and ¾ teaspoon citric acid or lemon juice. Slice the soft nuts thinly and drop quickly into boiling water to preserve colour. Do not remove skins. Boil the nuts for 40 minutes. Add sugar and citric acid or lemon juice; stir till dissolved. Bring to the boil and boil quickly for about 10–20 minutes or until it sets. It is best to make this marmalade in small quantities, but if using more than 225g of walnuts reduce the quantity of water to 425ml (¾pt) per 225g of nuts.

Walnut ketchup
Wash and prick all over 48 soft green walnuts. Put them in a large bowl containing 4½l (1qt) vinegar, 3 tablespoons salt, 1 clove of garlic and 120g (4oz) finely chopped shallots. Leave for ten days, stirring every day. Put the liquor into a preserving pan with a blade of mace, 12 whole cloves, 25g (1oz) whole pepper and 1 tablespoon anchovy essence. Simmer gently for 30 minutes, skimming occasionally.

174

Pour into clean bottles, cork and seal when cold.

Corn salad with walnuts

225g (½lb) corn salad (lamb's lettuce)
4 dessertspoons nut or other oil
2 dessertspoons lemon juice
1 tablespoon chopped mixed wild herbs
pinch of salt and paprika
120g (4oz) walnut kernels

Wash corn salad and soak in slightly salted water for 20 minutes. Rinse the leaves in lukewarm water and drain well. Mix together oil, lemon juice, herbs and seasoning, stirring well to break up oil. Halve or quarter the walnuts and add them to dressing. Mix in corn salad, turning over until well coated.

Walnut cream

To 225ml (8floz) of whipped cream add 3 egg yolks, 1 tablespoon fine sugar and a few drops of vanilla essence. Mix in 120g (4oz) ground walnuts, 1 teaspoon lemon juice. Lastly fold in the stiffly beaten egg whites.
   Serve chilled with fresh berries.

Steamed walnut pudding

75g (3oz) butter or margarine
75g (3oz) sugar
4 egg yolks
1 whole egg
grated peel of ½ lemon
120g (4oz) milled walnuts
120g (4oz) brown breadcrumbs
3–4 tablespoons top of milk or thin cream
4 egg whites
extra breadcrumbs for lining

Cream butter and sugar. Add 4 egg yolks, the whole egg, lemon peel and beat thoroughly. Add nuts, breadcrumbs and milk or cream. Fold in the egg whites beaten to a froth. Line a greased pudding basin with breadcrumbs, fill with mixture and steam for 1 hour.

Curried walnuts

50ml (2floz) olive oil or fine vegetable oil
1 tablespoon curry powder
1 tablespoon Worcestershire sauce
⅛ teaspoon cayenne pepper
275g (10oz) shelled walnuts

Shell but do not peel walnuts. Combine oil, curry powder,

175

Worcestershire sauce and cayenne pepper in a heavy skillet. When the mixture is very hot, add walnuts and coat thoroughly. Take off heat.

Line a baking tin with brown paper, pour in the nuts and bake in oven at 150°C (300°F, Gas 2), for about 10 minutes or until crisp.

Walnut-butter spread

50g (2oz) butter
120g (4oz) ground walnuts

1 tablespoon (or less) Worcestershire sauce

Cream butter until soft. Stir in walnuts and Worcestershire sauce.

Spread on brown bread, toast, biscuits or crackers.

Cheese salad with walnuts

75–120g (3–4oz) cream, Brie or Camembert cheese
1 tablespoon chopped mixed herbs
1 tablespoon chopped olives
½ teaspoon lemon juice

1 tablespoon single cream
halved walnut kernels to decorate
watercress, corn salad or lettuce leaves

Mix cheese with herbs, olives, lemon juice and cream until soft. Shape into balls and decorate each with 2 walnut halves.

Serve on chosen salad leaves.

Walnut cake

120g (4oz) butter or margarine
175g (6oz) brown sugar
1 heaped teaspoon ground cinnamon
1 tablespoon lemon juice
grated peel of one lemon
50g (2oz) finely chopped walnuts

2 yolks of egg
120g (4oz) flour
½ teaspoon salt
1 teaspoon baking powder
125ml (4floz) single cream
2 whites of egg, stiffly beaten
coffee icing

Cream together butter and sugar until fluffy. Stir in cinnamon and lemon juice with peel, then add the walnuts. Beat yolks in a separate bowl, beat in the sifted dry ingredients. Add cream and mix well. Combine the two mixtures, stirring until blended, and lastly fold in the whisked egg whites. Bake in moderate oven, 180°C (350°F, Gas 4), for 45 minutes.

Allow cake to cool before spreading with coffee icing, made with a lightly beaten egg white, about 225g (8oz) sifted icing sugar and a little instant coffee dissolved in a few drops of hot water.

9
WILD FOODS IN THEIR SEASONS

Throughout the four seasons of the year the wild plants of the countryside can provide an abundance of food for you to enjoy and it is free for the picking. Use these seasonal lists for at-a-glance information so that you will know the food plants to look for at a particular time of the year. Compile your own guide using these ideas in a basic list, and carry it with you when you go on a country walk or for a drive. For future reference, keep a special diary noting where and when the plants are found.

Use wild foods for an unusual picnic to take with you on your rambles. Make a thick nourishing soup of mallow leaves flavoured with wild herbs, and keep it hot in a thermos flask. Nibble salted beechnuts. Serve chickweed sandwiches and take a sustaining sea-spinach tart to eat cold. To finish eat candied chestnuts and fresh wild fruit with beech nut crescents.

Spring

Soups	Nettles, sorrel, dandelion, lady's smock, St George's mushroom, morels Flavourings—wild herbs, burdock juice Thickening—boiled mallow leaves
Green salads	Nettles, charlock, chickweed, daisy, plantain, scurvy grass, shepherd's purse Vinegar substitute—sorrel
Main course	St George's mushrooms, morels, *Boletus granulatus*, herb bennet root, orpine root, purslane, alexanders buds Flavourings—mixed herbs, tansy leaves
Cooked vegetables	Alexanders and thistle stems, hop and seakale shoots, samphire, marsh woundwort
Spinach greens	Charlock, daisy, ground elder, nettles, plantains, lady's smock, sorrel, willowherb
Puddings and sweets	Elderflowers, tansy Rennet substitute—nettles
Drinks and wines	Brooklime spring drink, scurvy grass, willowherb, dandelion flower wine
Preserves	Bottle, dry, freeze—mushrooms, herbs and green leaves Ketchups, sauces, pickles—St George's mushrooms, morels, boleti, samphire

Summer

Salads	Dandelions, chickweed, nettles, sea purslane, evening primrose root, borage flowers, wild herbs
Main course	Cep mushrooms including the following boleti:* *Boletus luteus, B. granulatus, B. bovinus, B. badius, B. piperatus, B. variegatus, B. subtomentosus, B. viscidus, B. elegans* chanterelles, parasol fungi, giant puffballs, field and horse mushrooms
Spinach greens	Sea spinach, sea purslane, fat hen, Good King Henry, sorrel, docks
Cooked vegetables	Alexanders, bulrush, bladderwrack, hops, seakale, thistle bracts, willowherb
Puddings and sweets	Raspberries, strawberries, cherry plums, elderflowers, elderberries, bilberries, blackberries, rowan berries, carragheen
Drinks and wines	Fruit juices, cups, syrups, vinegars—raspberries, strawberries, bilberries, blackberries, elderberries Cordials, wines, spirits, beers—elderflowers, elderberries, rowan berries, sloes, nettles, dandelions
Preserves	Bottle, freeze, dry—fruits, berries, mushrooms, herbs, green leaves Jams, jellies—soft fruits, elderberries, cherry plums, rowan berries Ketchups, chutneys, pickles—blackberries, elderberries, mushrooms and fungi

* Various edible boleti not included in Chapter 7 under ceps (p.130). Identify carefully with expert or good field guide.

Autumn

Breakfast	Porridge meal—couchgrass, common reed, silverweed On muesli—hazel-nuts, berries
Soups	Chestnuts, mushrooms and fungi
Salads	Corn salad, chickweed, marsh woundwort, orpine, saffron milk cap fungi Hazel-nuts, walnuts
Main course	Field and horse mushrooms, honey fungi, oyster mushrooms, most edible boleti to be found in summer
Cooked vegetables	Evening primrose, goatsbeard, marsh woundwort, pignut, orpine, silverweed, willowherb, thistles, burdock
Seeds for sprouters	Burdock, charlock
Seeds to eat raw	Bulrush, mallow
Puddings and sweets	Cranberries, hawthorn, medlars, rosehips, hazel-nuts, chestnuts, walnuts, almonds
Cakes and biscuits	Hazel-nuts, chestnuts, walnuts, almonds, beech nuts Flour substitute—fat-hen seeds, bulrush pollen, couchgrass root
Drinks	Juices, syrups—fruits and berries Coffee substitutes—dandelions, hawthorn, acorns
Preserves	Bottle, freeze, dry—fruits, berries, rosehips, mushrooms, nuts, roots Jams, jellies—barberries, blackberries, crab apples, cranberries, hawthorn, juniper Chutneys, pickles—bullace, elderberries, samphire, juniper

Winter

Breakfast	Same as autumn, sea lettuce
Soups	Chestnuts, mushrooms, dried roots and wild flavouring herbs
Salads	Corn salad, winter purslane, brooklime, blanched dandelion leaves, shepherd's purse
Main course	Blewits, oyster mushrooms, beefsteak fungi, Jew's ear, most boleti, laver, sea lettuce, chestnuts, walnuts, hazel-nuts
Cooked vegetables	Dandelion, earthnuts, silverweed
Sprouter seeds	Burdock, charlock
Puddings and sweets	Late blackberries, barberries, crab apples, hazel-nuts, chestnuts, walnuts, almonds
Cakes and pastries	Chestnuts, hazel-nuts, beech nuts Preserved fruits—hawthorn, bilberries
Sweetmeats	Chestnuts, hazel-nuts, walnuts, burdock stems
Drinks	Dried herb and leaf teas, dandelion coffee Preserved fruit juices and syrups
Preserves	Bottle, freeze, dry—boleti Pickles, ketchups—blewits, boleti, samphire

Menus for Spring

Spring soup
or
Hop shoots with melted butter

Kelp patties
with hawkbit salad and ground elder spinach

Elderflower fritters

*   *   *

Purslane salad
or
Badderlocks in butter sauce

Morel croquettes
with daisy greens and seakale stems

Lemon-flavoured carragheen mould

*   *   *

Alexanders stems
or
St George's mushroom soup

Grilled small mackerel with sorrel sauce
and willowherb greens

Tansy pudding

Menus for Summer

Samphire with melted butter
or
Bulrush stem salad

Cèpes en Provence
with fat-hen greens

Raspberry flummery
or
Ice cream and cloudberry sauce

*   *   *

Chanterelles and tomatoes

Sea-spinach tart with a mixed wild
green salad

Bilberry tart

*   *   *

Thistle-bract 'artichokes'
or
Fat hen with cheese

Parasol fungi en casserole with
creamed bladderwrack

Wild strawberry ice cream

Menus for autumn

Fried puffball slices with wedge of lemon

Cold roast mutton with sloe jelly
and creamed goatsbeard roots

Herb bennet-stuffed apples *or*
Fresh fruit salad in rosehip syrup

*   *   *

Individual mushroom soufflés *or*
Shepherd's purse slaw

Vegetarian nut roast with
braised silverweed roots and
burdock stems

Fresh blackberries and cream *or*
Baked medlars

*   *   *

Marsh woundwort salad *or*
Silverweed gruel

Mixed fungi pie *or*
Ceps omelette with
orpine root vegetable and
chickweed salad

Almond plum tart *or*
Crab apple and elderberry pie

Menus for winter

Corn salad with beetroot *or*
Chestnut soup

Blewit stew *or*
Nut croquettes
with dandelion greens

Rosehip tart *or*
Walnut cream pudding

*   *   *

Laver hors d'oeuvres

Roast pheasant and juniper preserve
with creamed salsify roots
and winter purslane salad

Sloe and apple pudding *or*
Hazel-nut ice cream with
chestnut biscuits

*   *   *

Sea-lettuce rolls *or*
Fried oyster mushrooms

Rabbit casserole with wild herbs,
brooklime greens and
blanched dandelion-leaf salad

Cherry plum pie

READING LIST

Agriculture & Fisheries, Ministry of, Bulletin No 23   EDIBLE AND
POISONOUS FUNGI
Belt, T.   WILD PLANTS FOR WINEMAKING   Amateur Wine-
makers Publications, 1978
Blamey, M., Fitter, R. S. & Fitter, A.   WILD FLOWERS   Collins,
1977
Ceres.   FREE FOR ALL *Weeds and wild plants as a source of food*
Thorsons, 1978
Dickinson, C. I.   BRITISH SEAWEEDS (The Kew Series)   Eyre &
Spottiswoode, 1963
Douglas, J. S.   ALTERNATIVE FOODS *A world guide to lesser
known edible plants*   Pelham Books, 1978
Eley, G.   WILD FRUITS AND NUTS   EP Publishing, 1976
Eley, G.   101 WILD PLANTS FOR THE KITCHEN   EP Publish-
ing, 1977
Gould-Marks, B.   PRESERVES *How to make and use them*   Faber,
1972
Hedrick, U.P. (ed)   STURTEVANT'S EDIBLE PLANTS OF THE
WORLD   Constable, 1972
Lange, M. & Hora, F. B.   GUIDE TO MUSHROOMS AND
TOADSTOOLS   Collins, 1963
Loewenfeld, C.   NUTS   Faber, 1956
Loewenfeld, C.   FUNGI   Faber, 1957
Loewenfeld C. & Back, P.   THE COMPLETE BOOK OF HERBS
AND SPICES   David & Charles, 1978
Mabey, R.   FOOD FOR FREE *A guide to the edible wild plants of
Britain*   Collins, 1972
Mabey, R.   ROADSIDE WILDLIFE BOOK   David & Charles, 1974
McClintock, D. & Fitter, R. S.   THE POCKET GUIDE TO WILD
FLOWERS   Collins, 1956

Masse, G.   BRITISH FUNGI AND LICHENS   Routledge, 1911

National Federations of Women's Institutes.   HOME MADE WINES, SYRUPS & CORDIALS   1954

Phillips, R.   WILD FLOWERS OF BRITAIN   Pan Books, 1978

Ramsbottom, J.   MUSHROOMS AND TOADSTOOLS   Collins, 1953

Reade, W. & Stuttard, R. M. (eds)   A HANDBOOK FOR NATURALISTS   Evans Bros with Council for Nature, 1968

Simon, André L.   FRUIT   Wine and Food Society, 1942

Svreck, Dr. M.   A COLOUR GUIDE TO FAMILIAR MUSHROOMS   Octopus, 1975

Szczelkun, S. A.   SURVIVAL SCRAPBOOK 2—FOOD   Unicorn Books, 1972

Urquhart, J.   FOOD FROM THE WILD   David & Charles, 1978

Yonge, C. M.   THE SEA SHORE   Collins, 1966

INDEX

Aegopodium podagraria (ground elder), 82-3
Agaricus (psalliota) campestris/arvensis (field mushroom), 137-43
Agropyron repens (couchgrass), 76
Alaria esculenta (badderlocks), 117-18
Alexanders *(Smyrnium olusatrum); stems,* 68-9
Alliaria petiolata (garlic mustard), 112
Allium ursinum/oleraceum/vineale (ramsons), 115
Almond *(Prunus amygdalus* spp), 158-61; almond plum tart, 160; cream-cheese salad with, 161; rosehip macaroons, 160-1
Anise cap *(Clitocybe odora),* 128-9; with spinach, 128-9; stuffing, 128
Anthriscus sylvestris (chervil), 111
Apple and sloe pudding, 66
Apples stuffed with herb bennet, 85
Arctium lappa (burdock), 72
Armillaria mellea (honey fungus), 143-5
Armoracia rusticana (horseradish), 112
Artemisia vulgaris (mugwort), 115
Auricularia auricula (Jew's ear), 145
Autumn; foods in season, 181; menus for, 185

Badderlocks *(Alaria esculenta),* 117-18; in butter sauce, 118
Balm (lemon balm) *(Melissa officinalis),* 110
Barberry *(Berberis vulgaris),* 37-9; juice, 39; marmalade, 38; preserve, 38-9
Basil *(Clinopodium vulgare),* 110-11
Beechnuts *(Fagus sylvatica),* 161-3
crescents, 163; oil, 162; salted, 163
Beefsteak fungus *(Fistulina hepatica),* 147-9
Beers, 35, 36
Beetroot with corn salad, 75

Bellis perennis (daisy), 76-7
Berberis vulgaris (barberry), 37
Berries, 24-5, 37-67
Beta maritima (sea beet), 98-9
Bilberry *(Vaccinium myrtillus),* 39-42
compote, 42; fritters, 41-2; tart, 41
Bishop's elder, *see* Ground elder
Black lovage, *see* Alexanders
Black potherb, *see* Alexanders
Blackberry *(Rubus fruticosus),* 42-5; cheese, 44; cordial, 44-5; pudding, 43, 44
Blackthorn, *see* Sloe
Bladderwrack *(Fucus vesiculosis),* 118-20 creamed, 119-20
Blaeberry, *see* Bilberry
Blewits *(Tricholoma* spp), 27, 129-30; in sauce, 130; stew, 130
Bluecap, *see* Blewits
Blueleg, *see* Blewits
Boleti, 27, 130-5
Borage *(Borago officinalis),* 111
Borago officinalis (borage), 111
Botanical Society of the British Isles, 15
Bottling wild food, 31-3, 40-1, 49-50
Bramble, *see* Blackberry
Brassica arvensis (charlock), 73-4
British Naturalists' Association, 15
British Trust for Conservation Volunteers, 15-16
Brooklime *(Veronica beccabunga),* 69-70 spring drink, 70
Bullace *(Prunus insititia),* 45-7; chutney, 46; gin, 46, 47; jam, 46-7
Bulrush *(Typha latifolia),* 70-1; stem salad, 71
Burdock *(Arctium lappa),* 72; candied, 72

Cabbage; and chestnut, 167; pickled white with junipers, 57
Candy and sweetmeats, 34

188

Index

Index

Forestry Commission, 15
Fragaria vesca (strawberry), 66-7
Freezing wild food, 28-9, 41, 44
French hales, *see* Rowan
Friends of the Earth, 16
Fruit, 24-6, 28-9, 37-67
  bottling, 31; drying, 31; freezing, 28-9;
  juices, 26, 34, 40; preparing and
  cooking, 24-6; syrup, 34; vinegars, 35
Fucus vesiculosis (bladderwrack), 118-20
Fungi, *see individual entries*

Garlic mustard *(Alliaria petiolata)*, 112
Gean, *see* Cherry plum
Geum urbanum (herb bennet), 84-5
Glasswort, *see* Marsh samphire
Goatsbeard *(Trapopogon pratensis)*, 80-2;
  roots, creamed, 82-3
Good King Henry, *see* Fat hen
Goosefoot, *see* Fat hen
Goutweed, *see* Ground elder
Green laver, *see* Sea lettuce
Grey mat, *see* Sea purslane
Ground elder *(Aegopodium podagraria)*,
  82-3; in tomato sauce, 83
Guide to picking wild plants, 11-12

Hale, *see* Hazel-nut
Halimione portulacoides (sea purslane),
  98-9
Hasketts, *see* Hazel-nut
Hawkbit *(Leontodon hispidus)*, 83-4
  salad, 84
Hawthorn *(Crataegus oxyacantha)*, 54-6
  berry wine, 56; jelly, 56
Haybox, 24
Hazel-nuts *(Corylus avellana)*, 167-72
  brandy snaps, 171-2; fruit jam with
  hazel-nuts, 172; fruit and nut pudding,
  170-1; ice cream, 171; preparation and
  cooking, 26; stuffed tomatoes, 172;
  uncooked nut cake, 171; vegetarian nut
  roast, 170; wild vegetables au gratin, 170
Hedge garlic, *see* Garlic mustard
Herb bennet *(Geum urbanum)*, 84-5
  stuffed apples, 85
Herb gerard, *see* Ground elder
Herbs, 21, 110-16
Hirneola auricular-judea (Jew's ear), 145
Honey fungus *(Armillaria mellea)*, 143-5
  mixed fungus pie, 144; and onions,
  144-5
Honey ware, *see* Badderlocks
Hops *(Humulus lupulus)*, 85-6
  shoots, 86; wine, 86
Horn of plenty, *see* Chanterelles
Horse mushroom, *see* Mushrooms, field or
  common

Horseradish *(Armoracia rusticana)*, 112
Humulus lupulus (hops), 84-5
Hurts, *see* Bilberry

Inedible nuts, 163, 164
Ink caps, 27-8
Iodine, 19
Irish moss, *see* Carragheen

Jack-by-the-hedge, *see* Garlic mustard
Jack-go-to-bed-at-noon, *see* Goatsbeard
Jams, 24-5, 33-4
Jellies, 25, 33-4
Jew's ear *(Auricularia auricula)*, 145
  salad of, 145
Juglans regia (walnut), 172-7
Juniper *(Juniperus communis)*, 56-7
  marinade, 56, 57; pickled white cabbage
  with, 57; preserve, 57
Juniperus communis (juniper), 56-7

Kelp *(Laminaria* spp), 123-4
  patties, 123-4
Ketchups, 35, 53, 174-5

Lactarius deliciosus (saffron milk cap),
  153-4
Lady's smock *(Cardamine pratensis)*, 87
  spring soup, 87
Lamb's lettuce, *see* Corn salad
*Laminaria digitata/stenophylla/
  saccharina* (kelp), 123-4
Lamium album (white dead-nettle), 90-1
Laver *(Porphyra* spp), 124-5; *hors
  d'oeuvre*, 125
Leaves, 68-109
Lemon balm, *(Melissa officinalis)*, 110
Leontodon hispidus (hawkbit), 83
Lepiota procera/rhacodes (parasol
  mushroom), 149-51
Liqueurs, 36
Livelong, *see* Orpine
*Lycoperdon gigantum/perlatum/
  gemnatum/caelatum* (puffballs), 151-3

Mallow *(Malva sylvestris)*, 87-8
Malus sylvestris (crab apple), 49
Malva sylvestris (mallow), 87-8
Marjoram *(Origanum vulgare)*, 112-13
Marsh samphire *(Salicornia herbacea)*, 96,
  98, 99; pickle, 99
Marsh woundwort *(Stachys palustris)*, 88-9
  root salad, 89
May, *see* Hawthorn
Meadowsweet *(Filipendula ulmaria)*, 113
Medlar *(Mespilus germanica)*, 57-9
  baked, 58; cheese, 58-9
Melissa officinalis (balm or lemon balm), 110

190

Index

Index

Salicornia herbacea (marsh samphire), 96, 98-9
Salsify (vegetable oyster), see Goatsbeard
Salvia verbenaca, 115
Sambucus nigra (elder), 52-4
Samphire (Crithmum maritimum), 95-6
Sauces, 35
Scurvy grass (Cochlearia spp), 96-7
Sea beet (spinach) (Beta maritima), 98
tart, 99
Sea fennel, see Samphire
Sea-girdles, see Kelp
Sea kale (Crambe maritima), 98, 99
Sea lettuce (Ulva lactuca), 125-6
rolls, 126
Sea purslane (Halimione portulacoides), 98, 99; salad, 99
Sea spinach, see Laver
Seaweeds, 117-26
Sea-wrack, see Bladderwrack
Seasonal guide, 178-86
Sedum telephium (orpine), 91-2
Shaggy caps, 27-8, see also Parasol mushrooms
Shepherd's purse (Capsella bursa pastoris), 100-1; slaw, 101
Silverweed (Potentilla anserina), 101-2
porridge, 102
Silybum marianum (milk thistle), 105-8
Sinapsis arvensis (charlock), 73-4
Sloe (Prunus spinosa), 65-6
and apple pudding, 66; gin, 65; jelly, 66; wine, 65-6
Smyrnium olusatrum (alexanders), 68
Society for the Promotion of Nature Conservation (Association of Nature Conservation Trusts), 17
'Soldiers', see Plantain
Sonchus arvensis/oleraceus (corn sow/common sow thistles), 105-8
Sorbus aucuparia/torminalis/latifolia/aria (rowan), 63-5
Sorrels, various (Rumex spp), 102-4
sauce, 104
Spanish chestnut, see Chestnut
Spring beauty, see Purslane
Spring; foods in season, 179; menus, 183
Stachys palustris (marsh woundwort), 88-9
Stellaria media (chickweed), 74
Stems, 68-109
Stonecrop, large, see Orpine
Strawberry (Fragaria vesca), 66-7
bowl, 67; mousse, 67; wild strawberry cup, 67; wild strawberry preserve, 67
Summer; foods in season, 180; menus, 184
Sweet chestnut, see Chestnut
Sweet Cicely (Myrrhis odorata), 116

Tanacetum vulgare (tansy), 104-5
Tangle, see Kelp
Tansy (Tanacetum vulgare), 104-5
pudding, 104-5
Taraxacum officinalis (dandelion), 77-8
Thistles, various, 105-8
Thyme (Thymus drucei), 116
Thymus drucei (thyme), 116
Tragopogon porrifolius/pratensis (goatsbeard), 80-2
Tricholoma gambosum (St George's mushroom), 155-7
Tricholoma personatum/nudum (blewits), 129-30
Twitchgrass (Agropyron repens), 76
Typha latifolia/angustifolia (bulrush), 70-1

Ulva lactuca (sea lettuce), 125-6
Urtica dioica (nettle), 90-1

Vaccinium myrtillus (bilberry), 39-42
Vaccinium oxycoccus (cranberry), 50-2
Vacuum flask, 24
Valerianella locusta (corn salad), 75
Vegetable protein, 18
Vegetables and plants
freezing, 29; preparation and cooking, 23-4
Verjuice, 49
Veronica beccabunga (brookline), 69-70
Vinegars, fruit, 35
Vitamins, 19, 21, 23, 42, 49, 60, 61, 72, 76, 88
Volatile oils, 21

Walnut (Juglans regia), 172-7
cheese salad with, 176; corn salad with, 175; curried, 175-6; green walnut marmalade, 174; ketchup, 174-5; steamed pudding, 175; walnut butter spread, 176; walnut cake, 176-7; walnut cream, 175
Waybread, see Plantain
Whin, see Bilberry
Whitebeam, see Rowan
Whitethorn, see Hawthorn
Whortleberry, see Bilberry
Wild cherry, see Cherry plum
Wild garlic, see Ramsons
Wild service tree, see Rowan
Willowherb (Epilobium angustifolium), 108-9
wines, 35-6
Winter; foods in season, 182; menus, 186; purslane (Claytonia perfoliata), 93
Woodland Trust, The, 17
Woodnut, see Hazel-nut

192